Donated by Prison Alliance
Write us a letter & enroll in
our PA Bible Study today!
PO Box 97095 Raleigh NC 27624

God created man and established his heart with kingdom values. Inherent in each of us is the kingdom value system waiting to express itself. Everybody is born with the values of God's kingdom. These values reflect in our culture, language and geographical location. You are born to live, win and succeed through the values you develop in life. God's value system develops the godly character the devil seeks to destroy. I wonder why there is nothing like charisma assassination. The devil cannot destroy your gift and potential but he can tarnish the image of the gifted person. If this happens, others will start to down-look, downgrade, disrespect and dishonor. Most people in our modern times spend most of their efforts developing their charisma instead of their character. Charisma elevates man. But Charisma does not sustain the person who is lifted until he develops quality character ethics.

This author deals with issues that confront the human soul which the devil uses to take advantage and to destroy the assignment man is called for. Spiritual Value System deals with issues related to your spiritual, emotional and psychological development. It offers guidance as to how to develop your charismatic and characteristic inclinations. Spiritual Value System is a life changing read.

Rev. Oppong Amoabeng
Resident Pastor, International Central Gospel Church
President, Kingdom For All Nations Outreach, Denmark

This is the most critical time for the church in all of its history, both in this nation, and in the nations of the world. The Church of Jesus Christ is at a point in our earthly world system where she must decide whether she's going to live by the world, or live by the Word. Julius Owusu captures the urgency of our dilemma with his book Spiritual Value System. Every believer who is serious about standing and living for God in these perilous times coming at the end of the age needs to get a copy of this book. It should be read over and over, until a systemic change occurs in their heart, bringing forth the expression of the kingdom of God in their lifestyle, choices and decisions.

Brondon Mathis
Director, International House of Prayer
Columbus Ohio, United States of America

This book is worth its weight in gold. It will stir your faith, prick your conscience, turn your life around for good and help define your prophetic inheritance in God. It is a winner any day.

Pastor Duke Ajieh
Country Coordinator for Norway
The Redeemed Christian Church of God

Julius Owusu understands that faith in God for victorious living entails more than knowledge. Propositional knowledge must become an inherent value that must be practiced. Only fervent practice of faith in God accrues transformation and true blessings. Three things are candid in the book – God must be the absolute priority, believers must be resilient not to trade our glorious inheritance for earthly and fleshly convenience, and the Word of God must be esteemed above all else. In sum, the book Spiritual Value System puts its readers in alignment with the perspective of God ….the kingdom of heaven is like unto a merchant man, seeking goodly PEARLS: Who, when he had found one pearl of great price, went and sold all that he had and bought it. If you put God first, you will be restored to first place.

Rev. Dr. Maclean Awuku
Vice President, Pilgrim Christian Ministries International
Italy

Spiritual Value System

Spiritual Value System

Esteeming Spiritual Things More than Fleeting Physical Things

Julius Owusu

SPIRITUAL VALUE SYSTEM
COPYRIGHT © 2013 – JULIUS OWUSU
First Edition 2013
Paperback ISBN: 978-1-62245-100-5
Ebook ISBN: 978-1-62245-101-2

Unless otherwise indicated, Scripture quotations are from the King James Version (KJV) of the Holy Bible. ALL RIGHTS RESERVED. No part of this book may be reproduced, shared in a retrieval system or transmitted in any form or by any means, electrical, mechanical, photocopy, recording or settings without prior written permission from the author and publisher.

Published & produced by:

LIFE SENTENCE Publishing, LLC
P.O. Box 652
Abbotsford, WI 54405

Edited by Donna Sundblad, and Yaw Frimpong Tenkorang

(Dream Enablers LTD: +233-20-6617983)

Cover design by Amber Burger

Printed by LIFE SENTENCE Publishing

For any information on the book or the author, please contact the publisher.

Printed in the United States of America

10 9 8 7 6 5 4 3 2 1

Dedication

I dedicate this book to my mentor Rev. Eastwood Anaba, Founder and President of Eastwood Anaba Ministries (EAM). Only heaven knows the tremendous impact your ministry has had on my life!

Contents

Dedication IX

Foreword.. XIII

Acknowledgement..XV

Introduction XVII

Ch. 1: Spiritual Value System Explained 1

Ch. 2: Cultivating a Daily Devotional Life 15

Ch. 3: Setting the Right Priorities... 29

Ch. 4: Seek the Main Thing, Get the Remaining, and Maintain the Main Thing 47

Ch. 5: Priorities, Blessings and Crumbs 57

Ch. 6: The World's Ways vs. The Word's Ways............................... 67

Ch. 7: Overcoming Addictions... 81

Ch. 8: Becoming a God-Addict 93

Ch. 9: Hungry and Thirsty for God.. 105

Ch. 10: Tips on How to Have a Spiritual Value System................. 117

About The Book... 125

About The Author 127

Foreword

We live in a physical world but it is imperative for every individual, believer or unbeliever to know the spiritual world controls the physical world. But how do we understand the spiritual as believers to make living in the physical a better place for us? Spiritual Value System offers the answers needed today.

In this life there are some things we must put first and through this wonderful book, the writer, Julius Owusu, shows us the need for placing great value on spiritual things; the things of God rather than the things of this world.

With great revelation, he shows us things that systematically expose our value system in life. He reveals how we can have a great intimacy with our Creator through cultivating a daily devotional life and explains the benefits of personal daily devotions.

He challenges believers to set right priorities in life and shows how essential it is for us to put God first in everything we do. As Matthew 6:33 says "But seek ye first the kingdom of God, and his righteousness; and all these things shall be added unto you." With an uncommon wisdom, he shows us the two kingdoms of life, which is the kingdom of God and kingdom of the Devil. The latter he calls the "World's Ways" and the former the "Word's Ways."

Finally, he explains that a great ingredient to a person's value system is what one is addicted to. His unique approach shows the processes that lead to addiction both good and bad and how it relates to your value system. He later admonishes us to become God-addicts.

Make this book one of your constant companions. Read and re-read it, get one for somebody and let's begin to prioritize spiritual things as they are more important than what meets the physical eyes.

Pastor Brian Amoateng
Founder, Brian Jones Outreach Ministries
London, England.

Acknowledgement

First of all, I thank the almighty God in a big way for giving me the vision and wisdom to write this book.

A very big thank you to my beautiful wife and friend for life, Princess, and our lovely children, Julian and Lois. I love you all so much!

Special thanks to my dad and mum, Mr. Francis Forbi and Madam Vida Kesse, and to my sisters: Christiana, Diana, and Faustina for your love.

My thanks also go to my good friend Yaw Frimpong Tenkorang, CEO of Dream Enablers Limited, for proofreading the manuscript of this book. Yaw, you truly did an excellent work. You have enabled my dream to come true as an author.

I want to thank my nephew Enoch Boamah for your great contribution to this book and pre-editorial skills.

I want to thank my pastor, Rev. Dr. Maclean Awuku, vice president of the Pilgrim Christian Ministries International, for believing in my gifts and talents and for your counsel and advice.

Also to my good friend Rev. Brian Amoateng; I appreciate your friendship and motivation a lot. Again, I am grateful to Bishop E. O. Ansah (KLM London), Pastor Oppong Amoabeng (ICGC Copenhagen, Denmark), Pastor Patrick Agyeman Dua (Fountain Gate Chapel, Adenta Commandos), Pastor Dickson Acheampong (Kingdom Embassy Int Church, Accra), and Pastor Johnny Tibu Darko (Fountain Gate Chapel, Berekum). Many thanks also go to Mr. Jeremiah Zeiset of LIFE SENTENCE Publishing and his entire team.

I am indebted to Mama Elizabeth Tekie, Mama Alice Opoku, Elder Elvis Ampadu, Elder Regina Boateng, Mama Ruth, and Mr. Sandy Dankwah for your diverse support and encouragement. My heart overflows with thanks to every member of Pilgrim Christian Ministries, Modena, especially, the youth. I love you all!

I appreciate Elder George Kissi Appiah and Mama Tina (London) and my friend Mr. Justice Mensah.

Introduction

For everything our senses encounter in the physical world, a parallel spiritual reality exists. In His teachings (and the Bible in general), Jesus uses physical things to teach spiritual truths or lessons, and in His parables, He used many physical things to represent or illustrate the spiritual. For example, He used the seed to represent the Word of God, soil to represent the human heart.

Just as our flesh wars against our spirits and vice versa, physical and spiritual things are also in keen competition. We are to choose and focus on spiritual things. They are more beneficial and important than physical things in every detail. Physical things are temporal but spiritual things are eternal. Unfortunately, we choose, give attention, and indulge in physical things or activities at the expense of the spiritual because the former are visible and more appealing to our senses. A clear case of out of sight, out of mind!

We are not just physical beings but spiritual beings as well. For that reason, there is the need to shift our attention from physical or earthly things to spiritual or heavenly things. We scramble to get things and struggle to get problems solved in the physical. We fail to understand that if we can deal with the problem in the spiritual first, it will either be a done deal or no longer a big deal in the physical. If we tackle it in the spiritual realm first, we can handle it in the physical realm.

This book will arouse your appetite for the things of God. It will teach you to stop chasing things of earth and to seek first the kingdom of God and His righteousness. This book will help make you the spiritual giant you ought to be. It will change you from being natural, carnal or religious to being spiritual and supernatural. You will be changed from being earthly minded to being heavenly or spiritually minded.

This is an easy-to-understand must-read for the believer and the unbeliever alike. The only difficulty you will encounter is that once you start reading, you won't be able to put this book down except to pray about it and then read on.

Just as various systems like the digestive, cardiovascular, nervous, reproductive, respiratory, circulatory, and musculoskeletal systems function in the body to give us life, *Spiritual Value System* works to make you spiritually alive.

Unbelievers will see the need to be born again. The backslider will return to the place of grace one more time, and the believer will move on to a new spiritual dimension in their walk with the Lord. If you're ready to stop being halfhearted and lackadaisical in your attitude towards the things of God, ready to pursue God with great inner tenacity, physical purity, moral integrity and spiritual intensity, *Spiritual Value System* is for you. Read *Spiritual Value System,* and you'll have a spiritual value system!

CHAPTER ONE

Spiritual Value System Explained

The dictionary defines a value system as "*a set of established values, norms or goals existing in a society.*"[1] It is also defined as "*the principles of right and wrong that are accepted by an individual or a social group.*"[2] It is "*any method or standard by which meaning or value is assigned to things.*"[3]

A variety of value systems exist amid different kinds of people. The believer, however, is supposed to have a strictly spiritual value system. Spiritual value system simply means esteeming spiritual things more than fleeting physical things. It places value on the things of God more than the things of this world. Better still, it sets your affection on things above. That is not to say physical or material things are unimportant. They are necessary, but when compared with spiritual things, they hold less value and relevance.

> *While we look not at the things which are seen, but at the things which are not seen: for the things which are seen are temporal; but the things which are not seen are eternal* (2 Corinthians 4:18).

---

[1] Value System. 2013. In *Merriam-Webster.com*. Retrieved July 1st, 2013, from www.merriam-webster.com/dictionary/value system

[2] Value System. 2013. In *TheFreeDictionary.com*. Retrieved July 1st, 2013, from www.thefreedictionary.com/value system

[3] Source unknown.

Value System Revealed

The Bible is full of men and women who displayed a spiritual value system. The choices they made, their words and works, confessions, statements, responses, and actions depicted lifestyles which placed value on spiritual things more than physical things. Now let me show you what reveals a person's value system, whether spiritual or not.

1. Who You Depend On Reveals Your Value System

From whom and where you seek help reveals much about your value system. Do you depend on God, man, or Egypt? The Scriptures say that *cursed are those who put their trust in mere humans,* (Jeremiah 17:5 NLT) and *woe to them that go down to Egypt for help* (Isaiah 31:1).

The Psalmist said *I will lift up my eyes to the mountains, where does my help come from? My help comes from the Lord; the Maker of heaven and earth* (Psalm 121:1-2 NIV). Just as the eyes of servants look to their masters' hands and expect it to visit their pockets, so the eyes of those whose value system is spiritual wait upon the Lord until He has mercy upon them. They lift their hands, lift up their eyes, and fix their heart on God for help, provision, and everything else. They know their supply comes from above. The question the king of Israel asked the woman who cried for help from the king teaches us that our total dependence must be on God.

> *The king replied, if the LORD does not help you, where can I get help for you? From the threshing floor? From the winepress?* (2 Kings 6:27 NIV).

One man whose answer and response shows he depended solely on Jehovah Jireh for provision and everything as a result of his value system is Abraham. In Genesis 14:22-23, this was what he said when the king of Sodom gave him an offer:

And Abram said to the king of Sodom, I have lift up mine hand unto the LORD, the most high God, the possessor of heaven and earth. That I will not take from a thread even to a shoe latchet and that I will not take anything that is thine, lest thou shouldest say, I have made Abram rich (Genesis 14:22-23).

Please be reminded that Abraham, at this stage, had not yet been blessed materially by God. If he rejected that offer after God fulfilled His promise to bless him materially that would have been no shock. It is easy to reject material wealth when you already have an abundance, but when you lack, the natural tendency is to grasp.

I like Abraham's (then Abram) reason for turning down the offer. Abraham refused it because he didn't want people to be confused as to who actually blessed him, God or man. Abraham knew people enjoy boasting about the slightest help offered, thus denying God all the glory in the process. People like to play God in your life; that is why you must pray God will manifest His blessing in your life.

> *If you refuse to turn away certain gifts and offers, you become a refuse dump where people throw their waste and junk.*

If you refuse to turn away certain gifts and offers, you become a refuse dump where people throw their waste and junk. Some people testify God has been good to them by giving them a financial breakthrough, and yet, they actually begged people for it. If you beg people to give you money, it's called alms, not God's blessings! Don't impose tax on people to give you cash and other things; trust God to touch them to bless you.

SPIRITUAL VALUE SYSTEM

And Saul also went home to Gilbeah; and there went with him a band of men, whose hearts God had touched (1 Samuel 10:26).

God blesses us through people. Nevertheless, let Him touch their hearts first. The heart of every man is in His hands, and He turns it wherever He wants. Anyone whose heart has not been touched by God to give cannot bless you. If they force themselves to give without their heart being touched by God, their motives are likely to be questionable. That is why it is indispensable for the Christian to pray without ceasing, because it is prayer that causes God to touch people's hearts to favor us.

Please, don't get me wrong. I am not saying reject every gift and offer. What I am emphasizing is our total dependence on God. Some people are so addicted to the help of man that in all situations their language is *how shall this be, seeing I know not any man?*– the words of Mary and the sick man at the pool of Bethesda. When we depend on God, He will give us favor and that favor will automatically extend to our dealings with men but not vice versa. *And Jesus increased in wisdom and stature and in **favor with God and men*** (Luke 2:52, emphasis mine).

> *Don't forget some gifts and offers are bribery in disguise.*

If you are a leader or a person in authority with people under you like a pastor or a manager, and you enjoy receiving gifts from those in your charge, your principle or duty to mete out discipline where and when necessary can be weakened or compromised. If you always accept things from their hands, it can influence your ability to correct them. Don't forget some gifts and offers are bribery in disguise.

> *He that is greedy of gain troubleth his own house but he that hateth gifts shall live* (Proverbs 15:27).

Don't feel compelled to accept every gift offered. Stay in prayer, for you don't have to grab every opportunity; it may be a trap. Seek God's will, because not every favor should be embraced. If men give with wrong motives, they will later demand you do their will rather than God's. Receive boldness to say a big NO to people who offer what appears to be good, but who have ulterior motives. Accepting gifts and offers from the wrong people can enslave, embarrass, or break you. Where God is taking you is so great He will be grieved if someone should one day get up and say, "that person, I helped or made him!" thus, taking all the glory in the end.

One example of a man who depended on God and refused to ask for help from another king was Ezra. He was torn between choosing human or divine protection, guard, and guidance; and he chose the latter.

> *Then I proclaimed a fast there, at the river of Ahava, that we might afflict ourselves before our God, to seek of him a right way for us, and for our little ones and for all our substance. For I was ashamed to require of the king a band of soldiers and horsemen to help us against the enemy in the way; because we had spoken unto the king, saying, the hand of our God is upon all them for good that seek him but his power and his wrath is against all them that forsake him* (Ezra 8:21-22).

The king would not have refused a squad of soldiers to escort Ezra and his people if he had requested, but Ezra simply refused to ask. It was shameful, in his opinion, to make such a request of the king. It would show reliance on human protection. However, he was not ashamed to publicly declare absolute dependence on God. Ezra and the Israelites made their boast in the Lord.

People whose value system is spiritual rely on God for practically everything. When what they expect from God is not forthcoming, they don't turn to man and ask for what God is capable of doing and doing better. Instead, they turn to fasting and prayers in order to seek the will of God. They understand when God said, *ask and it shall be given,* He meant asking Him not man. To the spiritually minded, it's a shameful thing to ask man for something God is capable of doing.

Boast in what God can do. When God calls a man, He anoints and empowers him for the task. It is a shameful thing to go for juju or black power. It is not a bad idea to adopt a child when the fruit of the womb is not forth coming after many years of marriage, but if you have told people your God is able to cause the barren woman to become a happy mother of many children, don't be quick to go for that option. The secret is in prayer, fasting, and waiting patiently on Him.

> *The secret is in prayer, fasting, and waiting patiently on Him.*

Be careful what you receive and from whom you receive it. Also be careful what you barter or exchange. A barter trade can either better your life or shatter it. Jacob and Esau did a barter trade, and while Jacob's life got better, Esau's life was shattered, making him bitter in the end.

Mentioning these twins brings me to my next point which centers partly on them.

2. What You Place Value On and Seek Reveals Your Value System

If ye then be risen with Christ, seek those things which are above, where Christ sitteth on the right hand of God. Set your affection on things above, not on things on the earth (Colossians 3:1-2).

People with a spiritual value system do not place value on material things more than God and His Word. When you consider the lives of Jacob and his twin brother, Esau, you realize the former had a higher spiritual value system in many ways. The obvious is the fact that Esau didn't value his birthright, and therefore swapped it for food from his brother.

And Jacob said, Sell me this day thy birthright and Esau said, I am at the point to die: and what profit shall this birthright do to me? And Jacob said, Swear to me this day; and he sware unto him: and he sold his birthright unto Jacob. Then Jacob gave Esau bread and pottage of lentils; and he did eat and drink and rose up, and went his way: thus Esau despised his birthright (Genesis 25:31-34).

After that exchange their father, Isaac, pronounced blessings upon Jacob. Yet when Jacob left home, he did not attempt to go with material things. How different Jacob is from the prodigal son who left home with his portion of goods just to squander his wealth on riotous living! Jacob did not say, "Now that I have the birthright give me a donkey, some cattle, gold, silver, and all the goods that fall to me, and let me go with them." Rather, the Bible tells us Jacob took only his staff which represented the guidance of the Holy Spirit. He went with the Word and prophecy via prayer which he had received in his spirit from his father.

Later, God blessed and increased him so much he expressed his gratitude to God in this way. *I am not worthy of the least of all the mercies, and of all the truth, which thou hast shewed unto thy servant;*

for with my staff I passed over this Jordan; and now I am become two bands (Genesis 32:10).

Those who don't have earthly wealth, but make the Word a priority, value their spiritual wealth. With your eyes on the Lord, it is not unusual in such cases, like Jacob, to overtake people in the world who cherish earthly wealth but who don't value the Word. If you have the Word without wealth, you have an advantage to overtake people in the world with wealth but without the Word. This is because the Word in the beginning will sooner or later become substance.

> *In the beginning was the Word and the Word was with God and the Word was God*
>
> *And the Word became flesh.* (John 1:1, 14a)

Another man who placed value on the Word was Job. In Job 23:12, he said *I have esteemed the words of his mouth more than my necessary food*. In Matthew 4:4 Jesus tells us both physical food and spiritual food (the Word) are necessary to live by, but Job reveals that between the two, one is more important – the Word.

> *Until the world exclaims we are too extreme, we have not yet esteemed the Word.*

The Word of God nourishes our spirits. In contrast, physical food feeds our bodies and is eliminated. We have three main daily meals: breakfast, lunch and supper. Apart from these, we also take in snacks and dessert. One can forgo the latter, but as for meals, one can hardly skip or forgo them unless for a special reason. What Job is saying is that he values, respects, and regards the Word of God more than his three square meals. He is willing to go days without physical food rather than go days without eating the Word of God. He understood spiritual starvation is more dangerous than physical starvation. Simply put, his value system was spiritual. He esteemed the Word. Until the world exclaims we are too extreme, we have not yet esteemed the Word.

F.F. Bosworth once said, "Most Christians feed their bodies three square meals each day but only feed their spirits one cold snack each week". Friend, I commend you to God and to the Word of His grace which is able to make you grow. Value the Word of God more than physical food if you want to grow spiritually. Everything shall pass away, but His Word shall never pass away. You ought to eat the Word, masticate it, digest it, and assimilate it for it to refresh your spirit and give you vitality.

Like Job, Mary also loved and valued the words that fell from Jesus' lips. She loved to sit at Jesus' feet to hear His Word and fellowship with Him, thereby developing her relationship with Him. In contrast, her sister, Martha, busied herself with the preparation of earthly food.

> *And Jesus answered and said unto her, Martha Martha thou are careful and troubled about many things. But one thing is needful and Mary hath chosen that good part, which shall not be taken away from her* (Luke 10:41-42).

3. What You are Willing to Let Go Reveals Your Value System

> *But what things were gain to me, those I counted loss for Christ* (Philippians 3:7).

In Philippians chapter 3, Paul points out that he previously had many things he could boast about; he had the outward sign of circumcision, proud heritage as a Hebrew Jew, held the most respected religious position in his time as a Pharisee, had great zeal against the church in defending the Jewish faith and obedience to the law.

Yet when he encountered the resurrected Jesus Christ on the road to Damascus, he was temporarily blinded so he could gain true sight. His eyes were opened to see that all the good things he achieved or possessed were obstacles to the best thing – a personal relationship with God through faith in Jesus Christ. After his life changing encounter with Christ, his value system changed. He counted his gains and achievements as dung.

You may count your position, qualification, wealth, career, business, reputation, possessions, and so on as gain, but if your value system is spiritual, you don't allow them to be a stumbling block to having a personal relationship with God and working with Him.

My good friend Rev. Brian Amoateng says that he put his degrees down to preach because of souls. Like a thermometer, you may have many degrees, but you must agree to put them down if God calls you to decree His Word. If God calls you to preach the gospel, don't be like the young rich ruler who could not entertain the idea of letting go his possessions to follow Jesus. Can you forsake all to answer the call? Can you resign from your high-profile position if God calls you into full-time ministry? If God calls you to preach the gospel, don't breach the command!

> *Like a thermometer, you may have many degrees, but you must agree to put them down if God calls you to decree His Word.*

4. What You Ask For Reveals Your Value System

My friend Yaw Frimpong Tenkorang explains this point well: "The things you ask for from God and even people reveal a lot about you. It reveals your priorities, vision, maturity or growth, and above all your value system. Children ask for toys, toffees, and the likes from their parents because they are children. As they grow, their values change so they stop asking for small things. King Solomon by virtue of his value system asked for understanding, and God saw it as the wisest request. What have you been asking God for? What have you been asking from influential and successful people when God allows your path to cross with theirs?"

> *In Gibeon the Lord appeared to Solomon in a dream by night: And God said, Ask what I shall give thee. Give therefore thy servant understanding heart to judge thy people, that I may discern between good and bad: for who is able to judge this thy so great a people? And the speech pleased the Lord that Solomon had asked this thing* (1 Kings 3:5, 9-10).

God granted Solomon's request and added unto him things he did not ask for: riches, wealth, and honor. If you ask God for the right things, He is able to give beyond what we ask or think (Ephesians 3:20).

The Bible says that when Solomon woke up, he realized it was a dream. When you know your dream in real life, you are focused even in your "dream life"! That is to say, even in your dreams, you pursue it, talk about it, ask the right questions, seek those things that will make your dream come true, stick to your values, and hold true to your priorities.

> *He made known his ways unto Moses, his acts unto the children of Israel* (Psalm 103:7).

You may wonder why God showed His ways to Moses, but to the children of Israel, His acts. The reason is that he simply asked for it in Exodus 33:13 as a result of his value system.

> *Now therefore, I pray thee if I have found grace in thy sight, shew me now thy way that I may know thee, that I may find grace in thy sight: and consider that this nation is thy people* (Exodus 33:13).

There is a difference between knowing God's ways and knowing his acts. Knowing the ways of God is knowing God. Knowing His acts is knowing what He does. The former are spiritually sound and mature in the things of God. The latter do not have their bearings and cannot navigate the things of God. When you know His ways, you will definitely know His acts, but when you know just His acts, you will not know His ways or Him, or the eternal life He offers.

5. Decisions and Confessions Reveal Your Value System

And if it seem evil unto you to serve the Lord, choose you this day whom you will serve; whether the gods which your fathers served that were on the other side of the flood or the gods of the Amorites, in whose land ye dwell: but as for me and my house, we will serve the Lord (Joshua 24:15).

Joshua succeeded Moses, and in that role, he led the Israelites through many conquests. In the above verse, he called on the people to remember all God had done for them, from deliverance in Egypt, forty years in wilderness, to their present moment of settling in the Promised Land. He then challenged them to make a decision to serve the Lord. As a true and exemplary leader, he led the way by being the first. He made this concrete decision to serve the Lord with his household as a result of his value system.

In the gospel of John, Peter, together with the disciples, made a similar decision. Jesus asked them who they wanted to follow, and Simon Peter responded in John 6:68: *Lord, to whom shall we go, you have the words of eternal life* (NIV). People who value their relationship with the Lord make such decisions and statements. If you have not yet made a conscious decision to serve the Lord, decide now, and if you have made the decision, do not turn back. Choose to train up your children in the ways of God. Choose to lead your household in the Lord. Just like Joshua, your decisions and actions will reflect your value system.

6. Places You Go Reveal Your Value System

In Psalm 84:10, the psalmist's value system is revealed by the place he loves and frequents: the house of God or the presence of God. He values being there more than any other place.

> *For a day in thy courts is better than a thousand. I had rather be a doorkeeper in the house of my God, than to dwell in the tents of wickedness* (Psalm 84:10).

In Psalm 122:1, David said, *I was glad when they said unto me; let us go into the house of the Lord.* "Tents of wickedness" refer to places where wickedness dwells, places where sin abounds, and the lack of God's presence. While God is omnipresent and His presence is everywhere, what is called His manifest presence is not everywhere. Why? Because He is holy and cannot come into contact with sin.

Like the psalmist, the believer should prefer going to church to going to the stadium to watch a game. When there is an important football match, it is common to find believers absent from church and glued to their television sets at home. This should not be so. Your spiritual life is more important than a live program on television.

> *The Word of God you hear from the podium is better for you than the mere entertainment value of watching the skill and flair of players at the stadium.*

The Word of God you hear from the podium is better for you than the mere entertainment value of watching the skill and flair of players at the stadium. Go to prayers instead of going to watch players. It's better to go to a revival meeting than to go and see a match between two rival clubs. Rather than going to support your favorite team in a local derby, you should go and support a brother or sister launching a debut book or album in your local church.

If your value system is spiritual, the match of your favorite team should not stop you from going into the house of the Lord to worship your Maker. After all, you can watch a replay later on television. If you value the spiritual, you must come to the place where you are satisfied to hear the results of games and not necessarily forfeit church to watch a match at the stadium or on television.

When your team loses, you will have *the sorrow of the world* which *worketh death* (2 Corinthians 7:10b) but in the presence of the Lord, *there is fullness of joy and at his right hand, there are pleasures for evermore* (Psalm 16:11b paraphrased).

7. The Choices You Make Reveal Your Value System

By faith Moses when he was come to years, refused to be called the son of Pharaoh's daughter; Choosing rather to suffer affliction with the people of God than to enjoy the pleasures of sin for a season; Esteeming the reproach of Christ greater riches than the treasures in Egypt: for he had respect unto the recompense of the reward. (Hebrews 11:24-26).

One person whose godly choices reveal his value system as being spiritual is Moses. When he came to the crossroad of choosing faith or fame, godliness or worldliness, godly suffering or worldly pleasure, fellowship with the people of God or fun with the people of the world, he chose the former. He turned his back on the pleasures of sin and chose to suffer afflictions with the people of God. He held in high esteem the reproach of Christ, greater riches than the treasures of Egypt.

Depending on God, valuing spiritual things, making right decisions, making right choices, and letting go of certain things must be done on a daily basis. To help us do that, we need to cultivate a daily devotional life.

CHAPTER TWO

Cultivating a Daily Devotional Life

When Christ died on the cross and the temple veil was torn in two from top to bottom, it was not merely intended to demonstrate the power of God. It indicated access to God was now permitted. It gave every believer in Christ an awesome privilege to come boldly and bodily into the presence of God. A daily devotional life is one way of enjoying this glorious privilege which leads to an intimate relationship with our Heavenly Father.

What is devotion or a quiet time with the Lord as it is otherwise called? It is sharing a private, intimate communion of fellowship with the lover of our soul, to deepen our relationship with Him.

When to Have Devotion

Setting aside this time with God has to be done on a daily basis. Why? Because God deals with us on a daily basis, and Satan also works against us on a daily basis.

> *Blessed be the Lord, who daily loadeth us with benefits, even the God of our salvation. Selah* (Psalm 68:19).

> *For that righteous man dwelling among them, in seeing and hearing, vexed his righteous soul from day to day with their unlawful deeds* (2 Peter 2:8).

Because God loads us with benefits daily, one purpose of our devotion is to daily thank Him. Also, the fact that we see and hear things that tempt us daily means we need to hide His Word in our heart and pray daily in order to overcome the numerous temptations thrown at us.

We tend to be very conscious of occasions like Christmas, Easter, our birthdays, and Sundays. For this reason, we wait until such occasions to thank God and be on guard against the onslaught of the enemy. Such occasion-conscious attitudes kill a God-conscious daily lifestyle and do not reflect a spiritual value system. If we are able to go to God and be with Him daily, then we can boldly say with Paul: *For which cause we faint not, but though our outward man perish, yet the inward man is renewed day by day* (2 Corinthians 4:16).

Devotion can be done or scheduled for anytime of the day, but in the morning before you get started into the busyness of the day is most ideal. Hence, it is popularly termed "morning" devotion.

> *The Lord GOD hath given me the tongue of the learned that I should know how to speak a word in season to him that is weary: he wakeneth morning by morning, he wakeneth mine ear to hear as the learned* (Isaiah 50:4).

Morning by morning, Isaiah says, the Lord God Himself wakes him up to speak and teach him His Word and ways, so he can be of tremendous blessing unto the weary, the weak, the discouraged, and the unsaved during the rest of the day. Brethren, the Holy Spirit wakes us to spend time with Him. The question is, do we respond? Are we willing to spend time alone with Him? If because the Holy Spirit speaks in a still, small voice, you cannot hear Him when He wakes you up, set an alarm! Apart from hearing Him, we also have the opportunity to speak to Him. In short, there is fellowship, communion, dialogue, intimacy, reciprocity, and so on.

> *My voice shalt thou hear in the morning. O Lord, In the morning will I direct my prayers unto thee and will look up* (Psalm 5:3).

The Benefits of Daily Devotions

The benefits of spending time alone with the Lord are enormous. Unfortunately, the enemy of our soul has succeeded in robbing countless Christians of this glorious privilege of loving on the lover of their souls reciprocally.

> *Come let us take our fill of love until the morning: let us solace ourselves with loves* (Proverbs 7:18).

The Bible is full of invitations from God the Father, God the Son, and God the Holy Spirit. Beginning in Genesis chapter seven with God's invitation for Noah and his family to come into the Ark to the last page of the last chapter in the last book of the Bible, God invites us to come to Him. The reason is that God seeks to fellowship and have an intimate relationship with man. The problem is that while many respond to the invitation of salvation, few honor the invitation to conversation which leads to intimacy. Acceptance of the gift of salvation should lead to a growing acquaintance.

> *The problem is that while many respond to the invitation of salvation, few honor the invitation to conversation which leads to intimacy.*

Many church folks do not deliberately and persistently spend quality time alone with the Lord. Perhaps the Devil knows that if he is able to defeat us in this area every morning of every day, then he will have a field day during the day. Beloved, if you do not have a devotional life, you have no idea what you are missing in your Christian life. If your former attempts have proven futile, I urge you not to give up.

I must confess that it is not easy to constantly spend time alone with the Lord. You may wrestle with your flesh which loves to sleep. The flesh will make you reach over and silence the alarm when it sounds. You may wrestle with your endless to-do list which competes for your time and attention, or you may struggle with many things around you which clamor for your attention. Discipline yourself by the power of the Holy Spirit to spend time daily with the Lord in prayer and the study of His Word.

It is sad to know that even some Christians do not say a common thank-you to the Lord after waking up from the world of sleep. They think that when they go to bed, waking up is automatic. They do not appreciate the gift of life and the opportunity to see another brand-new day. They have no idea that the One who neither sleeps nor slumbers is the One who gives His beloved sleep and sustains them in their sleep.

> *I laid me down and slept, I awaked for the Lord sustained me* (Psalm 3:5).

They rise up from bed, eat breakfast, drink some juice, listen to the news, and go out to their daily schedules. Their lifestyle is similar to that of the people of Israel at a point in history of which Paul warned us not to be like them.

> *Neither be ye idolaters, as were some of them; as it written, the people sat down to eat and drink, and rose up to play* (1 Corinthians 10:7).

The Israelites considered life and their spiritual lives for that matter to be like a game. A game is just a game, but Christianity is more than that. It is a titanic conflict against the forces of darkness! In a game, if you do not play well, you only become a loser, but in Christianity, if you are not serious and do not pray well, you become a casualty.

Before you take your breakfast, eat the Word, be filled with the wine of the Holy Ghost and pray. If you don't pray but play, you delay your break-through, you will fall prey to Satan, and your life will become a play or drama people will watch and laugh. When your life is void of miracles, you cannot avoid being ridiculed. I have made mention already that devotion is ideal in the morning. Spending time with Him in the early hours of the day strategically positions you to embrace His mercies and compassion which are new every morning.

> *Please listen: before you sit down to listen to the news at seven, kneel down to ask for the dew of heaven.*

> *And the angel that talked with me came again, and waked me, as a man that is wakened out of his sleep. And he said unto me, What seest thou?* (Zechariah 4:1-2a).

When the angel woke Zechariah up, the first question he asked him was, "What do you see?" When we wake up in the morning, what we see, hear, and do is very crucial in determining how the rest of the day goes. That makes the first minutes or hours after waking up very vital. A good foundation is important. If the foundation be broken, what shall the righteous do? When Zechariah described what he saw and asked the angel for explanation, the angel said he was seeing the Word of the Lord to Zerubbabel, that not by might, nor by power, but by the Spirit of the Lord, and that the great mountain before Zerubbabel shall become a plain, because though it's big, it's no big deal.

What do you see in the morning when you wake up? Who do you first talk to? Most people almost immediately after waking up are quick to watch and listen to news on television. Please listen: before you sit down to listen to the news at seven, kneel down to ask for the dew of heaven. The dew of heaven is the favor of God. Ask God to show you favor before you watch or listen to your favorite morning show. Before you hear something new in the news, have an encounter with your heavenly Father and ask Him to do something new in your life. For all you know, there is barely something new in the news. Choose to make a date with the Date you have with the Lover of your soul before you listen to news update. Cast your burdens unto Him who cares before you listen to the news broadcast and become preoccupied with the cares of life.

Before you hear the weather forecast to know whether it will rain or not, ask the Lord to reign in your life. Ask God to let the face of His Son shine on you before you find out whether there shall be sunshine. I know most people hate that white substance called snow, but when you ask Him, His blood can wash you and make you as white as snow. Expect showers of blessings.

Child of God, glean biblical truths daily before you glance through the pages of any daily newspaper. The Bible is fresher than tomorrow morning's newspapers. It's evergreen, so glean the truths therein. I am not against listening to the news to be current, informed, and up to date regarding world affairs and happenings. I am against letting it be your priority. To hit the nail right on the head, I must point out that it is better to have the news blacked out than to go out without the Word! The former will make your head blank regarding world issues, but the latter will make your heart empty, out of which come the issues of life.

What the news reports is usually bad news which brings fear and hopelessness. In contrast, the Word will increase your faith. You need the good news in a world of bad news – floods, earthquakes, terrorist attacks, famines, murders, diseases, economic recession, air and water pollution. The list is endless.

After you have eaten the Word and emerged from your prayer closet, you can boldly say the Lord is mightier when you hear heart-wrenching breaking news. When you hear there is famine and that people have resorted to begging, your confession will be, "I will trust in the Lord instead of begging." You can declare there is a lifting up when you hear there is a casting down. You shall say you are exempted from calamity and disaster for the Lord is your protector when you hear thousands and ten thousands are falling everywhere. In short, you will respond to any evil report with the Word.

When you fail to seek God in the morning, do not expect Him to be found when the need arises during the day. In fact, it is only when you dwell in the secret place of devotion that the wonderful promises in Psalm 91 can be your portion.

Practical Hints

A devotional pattern that will work for someone may not work for another since we all have different schedules, status etc. However, the following general guidelines can be followed by any fellow to ensure successful devotions.

- Find a regular quiet place and time to meet with the Lord.
- Get a Bible, notebook, pen, and a devotional guide or Bible reading plan.
- Avoid distractions in order to concentrate and focus on God. That may mean you have to turn off your phone, switch off the television, etc.
- Forget about any problem you may have and focus on God.

- If you like, play soft Christian worship songs.

Surely, I have behaved and quieted myself as a child that is weaned of his mother: my soul is even as a weaned child (Psalm 131:2).

It helps a lot to use a devotional guide. Wondering and guessing where to read is not good. Devotion must be purposeful.

Learn to Sit – In Spite of the Busyness of Going About the Kingdom Business

Jesus frequently visited Martha, Mary and Lazarus in their home in Bethany. During one such visit, Martha was preoccupied with serving while Mary sat and talked with Jesus. Let's take lessons from what transpired on a different occasion.

Then Jesus six days before the passover came to Bethany where Lazarus was which had been dead, whom he raised from the dead.

There they made him a supper; and Martha served: but Lazarus was one of them that sat at the table with him. Then took Mary a pound of ointment of spikenard, very costly, and anointed the feet of Jesus, and wiped his feet with her hair: and the house was filled with the odour of the ointment (John 12:1-3).

On this particular occasion, they all prepared supper for Him. Afterwards, Martha served and Lazarus (whom He raised from the dead) just sat at the table with Him. *They made him a supper* suggests they all contributed money, used their energy, and exhibited their culinary skills to ensure palatable food was on the table for Jesus. They made Him a supper because God demands our substance, and Martha served because He requires our service. Though we do well to serve and give from our substance, we more often than not forget to do what Lazarus did – sit at the table with Him.

Giving and serving can sometimes be flamboyant, lofty and showy – attracting much attention – while "sitting" can be so lowly it is hardly noticeable. It is for this reason Mary and Martha are always considered protagonists, thus, taking center stage while their brother Lazarus hardly attracts any attention. But what Lazarus did, as simple as it was, teaches a great deal to any Christian or servant of God busy for the Lord.

More often, we get caught up in the busyness of serving Him and the cheerfulness of giving to Him bountifully from our substance, but we fail woefully to sit at His feet. He needs us to sit at His feet because it gives Him the opportunity to fellowship with us and to shower His love on us. As we offer Him our substance and service, we should not forget to offer Him our selves; we must offer our time for Him to imbed or instill His divine nature and likeness in us.

> *Giving and serving can sometimes be flamboyant, lofty and showy – attracting much attention – while "sitting" can be so lowly it is hardly noticeable.*

It agitates me when I don't have enough time to fellowship with the Lord as I ought to. As we advance in ministry, many doors open to serve our Savior in numerous capacities. Travel itineraries to minister become loaded with conferences to preach and seminars to speak at; or there is a big and ever-growing church to pastor, and other such opportunities. Even with a full schedule, He expects us to sit and fellowship with Him.

We can be busily preaching the whole world out of hell, but He still wants us to sit at His feet. We can work long hours in order to excel in giving, but He wants us to sit at His feet. Our busyness for Him is no excuse.

> *And as thy servant was busy here and there, he was gone. And the king of Israel said unto him, so shall thy judgment be; thyself hast decided it* (1 Kings 20:40).

As servants of the most High God, we can be very busy for Him, and there is nothing absolutely wrong with being busy doing the work of the Lord. What is wrong is for us to preoccupy ourselves with our own agenda without doing the work of Him who called us. It has been said that the acronym BUSY represents "Being Under Satan's Yoke." When you are busy doing what God has called you to do, you are not under Satan's yoke, but he can choke your personal relationship with the Lord through negligence.

In fact, before His departure, Jesus told His disciples, and us for that matter, to occupy till He comes. That implies He wants to come and meet us as we are busy preaching the gospel, busy healing the sick, busy casting out demons, and busy walking in total dominion. As you get busy here and there, going here and there, doing this and that for the Lord, and in the name of the Lord, you should be careful to spend time with the Lord. The busyness of doing the kingdom business should not hinder your one-on-one fellowship with the Father. Preacher, you are propagating the gospel in order to depopulate hell and populate heaven; you need to spend time alone with God in order to recuperate.

Whether we serve Him or give Him our substance, He wants us to sit at His feet. I love one meaning of sit which is "to be located or situated." It does not matter how busy we are for the Lord, He wants us to be located in His presence, either alone with Him or in a church setting. I mentioned church because there are folks who erroneously think that so long as they give a lot to the Lord, they can absent themselves from church to go and work in order to earn more to give.

I am glad Lazarus was linked with the sitting, because he was dead once and Jesus raised him from the dead. Those who remember they were dead in sin and trespass know the importance of sitting. Those who remember what the Lord has done for them sit at His feet. For some people, God just found them and picked them from the surface of the earth. For others, He had to dig long and mine deep before He could get hold of them. If you fall into the category of the latter, you ought to know the importance of sitting at His feet.

Those who "sit" are those who remember where they were and how far the Lord has brought them. Those who "sit" are those whose total dependence is on Him; they recognize Him as their only source of power, and without Him, they can do nothing. Those who "sit" are ready to learn and listen to instructions, so they will not do things their own way.

The servant in the Scripture above gave an excuse. He said, *while I was busy here and there.* We are often quick to give this kind of excuse, justifying the fact that we are unable to spend time alone with God in the study of His Word and prayer.

Jesus always had an intense and busy day during His earthly ministry, and yet, He found time to fellowship with the Father. He set Himself to pray throughout the night on several occasions. At times, He would sleep, wake up in the middle of His sleep, and go to a solitary place to pray and fellowship with His Heavenly Father.

A great while before day, he went out, and departed into a solitary place, and there prayed (Mark 1:35).

Jesus' sustained success in ministry stemmed from His continual and persistent fellowship with the Father. Where we push, He only touched; where we scream and shout, He only whispered; where we pray long prayers, He only spoke words and phrases, and there were results. At certain times, He spoke no words at all. The glory in His face was enough to make demons scream and expel from their victims.

Jesus promised us that we would do the works He did and even greater. Apparently, it stands to reason that we have no option than to pray for more hours privately like He did, if not more.

> *Verily, verily, I say unto you, He that believeth on me, the works that I do shall he do also; and greater works than these shall he do; because I go to my Father* (John 14:12).

Refusal to spend time with Him affects our effectiveness in ministry. When Peter prayed and waited on God for ten days, three thousand souls got saved in a day when he preached one sermon. Today we pray for a day and preach for ten days continuous, and the results have been nothing to write home about.

There is danger in refusing to sit at the Master's feet. Jesus asked a thought-provoking question in Mark 8:36; *what shall it profit a man if he gain the whole world, and lose his own soul?* We normally interpret this Scripture by saying we are great losers if we gain the world's riches, fame, power, etc. and end up in hell. I want to ask a question from Jesus' question; could it be possible that we can win every soul in the world for Him and yet lose our own souls in the end simply because we failed to take time to develop our personal relationship with the Lord? The apostle Paul warned:

> *Where we push, He only touched; where we scream and shout, He only whispered; where we pray long prayers, He only spoke words and phrases, and there were results.*

Wherefore let him that thinketh he standeth take heed lest he fall (1 Corinthians 10:12).

Again the Bible says that in the last day, Jesus will tell some people to depart from Him. He does not know them, and they are workers of iniquity. I want to ask yet another question, thought-provoking one of course; could it be that He can tell us to depart from Him on that day, not because we worked iniquities per se, but simply for the fact that He didn't know us because we regularly failed to show up in His presence? In reality we will not go to hell if we truly know him, but if we truly know him, won't it be reflected in the time we spend with Him?

CHAPTER THREE

Setting the Right Priorities

The word *priority* means "something that is given special or prior attention." It is also "the right to precede others in order, rank, *or* privilege." To set priorities, therefore, is to put several things, such as problems, activities, interests, and tasks, in order of importance, so the most important ones are dealt with first.

Setting priorities is vital because some things or activities are more important than others. Some issues are more urgent than others, some matters are more pressing than others, and some ventures are more lucrative than others. While some deadlines need to be met at all cost, others can wait in the pipeline. While some things can wait, other things cannot. Some things can be overlooked; some need to be looked at immediately.

Having priorities in your life guides you in how best to invest time, energy, attention, resources, and money. It is good for individuals as well as corporate organizations to set priorities, because it results in maximum efficiency, excellence, and fulfillment. An organization that wants to gain a greater share of the market or become a market leader in its field of operation makes customer satisfaction their top priority. They put the customer first and seek to satisfy him with quality goods and services that meet or surpass their tastes and preferences. This way, they are able to stay in competition in today's rather competitive business world.

Some people set priorities for their lives and say "business before pleasure!" These people will not leave their business or jobs and go and have pleasure or fun when they need to be working. They are so diligent in business or with their work that they would say "pleasure can wait!" Call them workaholics, but they have disciplined themselves to put their priorities in the right order. You ought to know when to work and when to go for a walk, when to endure the pressures of work and when to enjoy pleasure after work, when to work overtime and when to have a nice time, when to go about your vocation and when to go for a vacation.

The God of Priorities

We can see from creation that God is a God of priorities. He could have created everything at once, but He set priorities and knew what to create each day. He did not go about things haphazardly. Because light is one of the first resources needed to create something, He said let there be light and there was light. God saw that the light was good, and He divided the light from the darkness. The Bible mentions that the day and night were the first day.

Before every human being comes into being, everything for his well-being is made ready, waiting for him.

Adam and Eve were not created last because they were least important in all the creations of God. They were created last because all God created was for their exclusive enjoyment. If God had created Adam and Eve first, they would have experienced a great deal of lack. Before every human being comes into being, everything for his well-being is made ready, waiting for him. All the creation of God was spoken into existence with the exception of man. When it got to his turn, God said let Us create man in Our image. This suggests the Godhead took time and patience to form, fashion, and design man, and that explains how important man is.

It is vital, however, to note that in setting priorities, sometimes the most important are deliberately reserved to be done or attended to last. For example, in sports, beauty pageants, and other competitions, the second runner-up is awarded first, followed by the first runner-up and finally the winner. You realize the winner receives the most attention, and the biggest reward or prize compared to the others, though she is the last to be crowned. In soccer and other sports tournaments, the game to determine third- and fourth-place teams is played before the grand finale which determines who takes home gold or the trophy at stake and the second-place team. Final matches that determine the championship receive unmatched publicity and media hypes. In this case, it is last, and it is the most important.

Having said that – how important or less important something is – is determined by the amount of time, money, energy, effort, attention, and so on is invested into that thing, but not merely whether it's handled first or last.

Regarding priorities, some people teach that God needs to be our top priority. Others also are of the view that we should let God set our priorities. While both schools of thought are not wrong, I will say that when the physical or natural conflicts with the spiritual or the supernatural, we must prioritize the latter. Right priorities are about elevating spiritual things to the top and relegating earthly things to the bottom.

My aim is not to give you a long list of what things should be first, second, third, or last. My aim is to help you put spiritual things above physical things. One man who did that was Isaac.

The Priorities of Isaac

The man began to prosper, and continued prospering, until he became very prosperous; for he had possessions of flocks and possessions of herds and a great number of servants. So the Philistines envied him (Genesis 26:13-14 NKJV). The envious Philistines were so upset that they filled all of Isaac's wells and king Abimelech told Isaac to leave simply because he was mightier than they. Isaac moved from one place to another, and faced opposition and conflict, until he came to Beersheba.

According to Genesis 26:23-25, on the night he arrived in Beersheba, God appeared to Isaac and gave him words of assurance and promise, after which he immediately set priorities for his life. God assured him of His presence and promised to bless and multiply him for his father Abraham's sake. Isaac understood immediately that for God's promises to come to pass in his life, he needed to put things right in his life. Many people have numerous promises from God and have received great prophecies, and wonderful visions which have not yet materialized simply because they have failed to set right priorities.

> *And he went up from thence to Beer-sheba and the LORD appeared unto him the same night and said, I am the God of Abraham thy father: Fear not, for I am with thee, and will bless thee and multiply thy seed for my servant Abraham's sake. And he builded an altar there, and called upon the name of the Lord, and pitched his tent there: and there Isaac's servants digged a well (Genesis 26:23-25).*

He Built an Altar and Called Upon the Name of the Lord - Devotion and Prayer

After God's promise to Isaac, his first set of priorities were devotion and prayer. Isaac built the altar, so he could have his devotion. What is an altar? An altar is a place designed or separated for worship unto

God, a place of fellowship with God. It is a place where praises and prayers are rendered unto God. Men of God in the Bible like Moses, Abraham, and Solomon built altars for God.

Isaac built the altar so he could go into the presence of God to have his devotion, spend time in worship, and commune and fellowship with God. He desired to have intimacy with God. God had assured him that He was with him, but he understood that for him to retain the presence of God, he needed to constantly abide in His presence and worship and fellowship. As he went to the altar, he called upon the name of the Lord. That is prayer. The Bible says *call unto me, and I will answer thee, and show thee great and mighty things, which thou knowest not* (Jeremiah 33:3).

Apart from prayer signifying our total dependence on God, Isaac understood that for God's promise to come to pass in his life, it would take prayer. He knew he had to be diligent in prayer in order to bring God's promise into physical and visible manifestation. Many times people who have God's wonderful promises play instead of pray, thinking those things God has promised will fall like ripe chilies.

When the Lord told Elijah in 1 Kings 18:1 that rain would come, Elijah did not just relax and expect the rain to fall. Rather, he began to pray persistently. In fact, the promises of God must be the basis for any prayer. The same is true with prophecies. A prophecy gives direction to your prayers.

He Pitched His Tent There and His Servants Dug Out a Well: Accommodation and Business

Isaac's second set of priorities were accommodation and business. He pitched his tent so it could serve as a dwelling place or a place of accommodation for him, and the well was dug so they could do business. It was done not only for domestic purpose but also for commercial and irrigational purposes.

Take note that he pitched a tent; he did not build a house. A house or building signifies permanence, but a tent speaks of temporariness and detachment. Isaac pitched his tent before he dug the well to do his business. If it was a house he built, it should have been the other way around.

> *Prepare thy work without, and make it fit for thyself in the field; and afterwards build thine house* (Proverbs 24:27).

This verse speaks of priorities, that your work be established before you build your house. It is wisdom. It is alright to rent today and build or buy later. Pitching a tent is, in a way, equal to renting a place of accommodation. Both denote temporariness.

In order to pass through untouched, we must remain detached from this world.

Like Isaac, we must know we are in this world temporarily. Here is not our home. As Christians, we are strangers and pilgrims passing through this world. In order to pass through untouched, we must remain detached from this world.

> *Dearly beloved, I beseech you as strangers and pilgrims, abstain from fleshly lusts, which war against the soul* (1 Peter 2:11).

By these examples, we see Isaac placed spiritual things and activities first and placed physical or material things second. This indicates Isaac valued spiritual things and activities more than their earthly counterparts. He placed a high premium on devotion and prayer – more than accommodation and business.

For most people, priority lists are the other way round. Instead of devotion and prayer being placed before accommodation and business, we place material things on top of our list and relegate the things of God to the bottom. Many have no value for spiritual things. We don't put God, and for that matter the things of God, first in our lives. Materialism is our preoccupation. All our time, energies, and efforts are geared toward material prosperity and gains. Simply put, we have our priorities in reverse.

If that is the case, we need to rewrite our priorities and put first things first. We need to set our priorities right in life – to set our eyes on things above.

First Things First

As I mentioned earlier, God is a God of priorities, and He wants us to set right priorities. Jesus always emphasized placing first things first in His teachings. When the Lord spoke about giving, warned against hypocrisy, touched on how to be blessed materially, revealed the signs of His coming, and so on, He emphasized putting first things first.

God tells us how to put first things first, and what that first thing ought to be. He warns us of the consequences if we don't prioritize, using illustrations we can apply to real life.

The Bible gives us examples of this:

> *Therefore, if thou bring thy gift to the altar, and there rememberest that thy brother hath ought against thee; Leave there thy gift before the altar, and go thy way; First be reconciled to thy brother, and then come and offer thy gift* (Matthew 5:23-24).

Jesus was saying that we should give priority to reconciling with our brother over the offering of our gift to the Lord. This is because broken human relationships can hinder our relationship with the Lord. Obedience is better than sacrifice. Giving a sacrifice or gift to God is very important to God. He demands it from us. His Word says we should not come before Him empty-handed. His Word commands us to bring our tithes, offerings, first fruits, and ultimately give our bodies as a living sacrifice.

For God to demand giving and for Him to say before you give you should restore broken relationships means we should not take the latter lightly. We cannot claim to love the Lord we do not see and hate our brother we do see. Loving your brother is supposed to be easier because you see him.

> *If a man say, I love God, and hateth his brother, he is a liar: for he that loveth not his brother whom he hath seen, how can he love God whom he hath not seen* (1 John 4:20).

When someone offends you, under normal circumstances, the onus is on that person to come to you and apologize. But in our text, Jesus meant you who have been offended to initiate peace. That is because our gospel is a "go to the world gospel." We are not to wait for them to come; it is our responsibility to take the first step and initiative. Do not wait for the needy to come and tell you their problems before you help. Go to them and inquire about how you can help. The Good Samaritan went to the wounded and half dead man and not vice versa. Do not wait for the world to come to church or into the kingdom. Go and preach to them. Anytime the Bible uses "go," it is a command.

> *And why beholdest thou the mote that is in thy brother's eye, but considerest not the beam that is in thy own eye? Or how wilt thou say to thy brother, Let me pull out the mote out of thine eye, and, behold, a beam is in thine own eye? Thou hypocrite, first cast out the beam out of thine own eye; and*

then shalt thou see clearly to cast out of the mote out of thy brother's eyes (Matthew 7:3-5).

When Jesus talked about taking the plank out of our own eyes before seeing clearly to remove the speck out of our brother's eye, he was referring to having the right priority.

A standard aircraft announcement has been used to explain the above Scripture. What they will tell you is that when the oxygen masks drop down, passengers must put on their own mask before trying to help others. If we fail to do so, we will lose consciousness. In that case, we would be of no help to others.

What we see when watching others depends on the purity of the window through which we look. Remove the plank out of your eye so you can see well enough to remove the speck out of your brother's eye. If you can clean your lens, you can see well.

Applying Wisdom vs. Employing Weapons of Warfare

Jesus told a parable of a tower-builder and a king who was contemplating going to war.

> *For which of you, intending to build a tower, sitteth not down FIRST, and counteth the cost, whether he hath sufficient to finish it? Lest haply, after he hath laid the foundation, and is not able to finish it, all that behold it begin to mock him, Saying, This man begin to build, and was not able to finish. Or what king, going to make war against another king, sitteth not down FIRST, and consulteth whether he be able with ten thousand to meet him that cometh against him with twenty thousand? Or else while the other is yet a great way off, he sendeth an ambassage, and desireth conditions of peace. So likewise, whosoever he be of you that*

SPIRITUAL VALUE SYSTEM

forsaketh not All that he hath, he cannot be my disciple (Luke 14:28-33, emphasis mine).

You realize that both ventures Jesus mentioned are very important. In building a tower a lot of money, time, and labor will be invested. Going to war is also a matter of life and death. The lives and destinies of people and perhaps a whole community, city, or nation may be at stake. It's for this reason the right thing must be done to prevent victims and the defeated from saying, "had I known."

Now, the key word in this passage is the word *first*. You ought to sit down FIRST! It means sitting down to plan must be the top most priority. If sitting down must be first, then something else must be second, third, fourth, and so on depending on importance, urgency, and the like. This is an example of priorities.

> *Casual behavior brings casualties. Haphazard behavior leads to hazards.*

"Sitting down" suggests that time must be invested brainstorming, exploring, and planning. It is not something to be done casually or haphazardly. Casual behavior brings casualties. Haphazard behavior leads to hazards. As the saying goes, "If you fail to plan, you plan to fail."

Jesus pointed out that in the first instance, failure to set priorities leads to failure and, eventually, ridicule or mockery from people. When you make a wise attempt at something and you fail, you receive encouragement from people. When you make a wise attempt at something and you succeed, you receive applause and praise from men. When you commit blunders in attempting to do something because of lack of planning, you receive ridicule. You will be mocked and made fun of. Folks will love you, laugh with you and be your fans when you succeed, but when you fail, they will laugh at you and make fun of you. Sometimes though, success attracts hatred and jealousy.

Receive grace to finish anything you start – your Christian life, marriage, business, project, education and so on! He who began a good work in you will bring it unto completion! Your hands started it, and your hands shall finish it!

If your enemies are rejoicing because you are stuck, you failed or have fallen as a result of a blunder you could have avoided. Look at the Devil, eyeball to eyeball, and declare this to him:

Rejoice not against me, O mine enemy, when I fall, I shall arise; when I sit in darkness, the Lord shall be a light unto me (Micah 7:8).

Most often we despise the wisdom of sitting down first to count the cost, plan, or strategize. Then after we have committed blunders and encountered defeats, we try to undo the mistakes and make amends by engaging in spiritual warfare. I must say that it is no coincidence that immediately after Jesus mentioned the wisdom and necessity of sitting down first in the case of the tower-builder, he touched on a king contemplating a war.

Most of the battles we fight in life are as a result of our failure to apply wisdom in the first place. We employ our weapons of warfare because we failed to apply wisdom. We fail to pay heed to counsel, so we end up praying to cancel the works of the Devil. If we apply wisdom to begin with, we will definitely avoid some battles in life.

Wisdom is better than weapons of war: *but one sinner destroyeth much good* (Ecclesiastes 9:18, emphasis mine).

The above Scripture points out clearly and emphatically that wisdom is better than weapons of warfare. It is far better to apply the wisdom of sitting down first in any venture than to employ your weapons of warfare later after a disastrous consequence. "Prevention is better than cure" goes the saying, and the Bible says wisdom preserves.

> *Wisdom is a shelter as money is a shelter, but the advantage of knowledge is this; wisdom preserves those who have it* (Ecclesiastes 7:12 NIV).

To apply wisdom is to apply God's Word. Thus, you sit when the Word says sit, you go when the Word commands you to go, you watch and pray as the Scripture admonishes. Jesus referred to the Word of God as the wisdom of God (Luke 11:49). He quoted Scripture after saying, *"therefore also said the wisdom of God."* Paul acknowledged Timothy's wisdom by saying it was as a result of the Holy Scriptures he had known from childhood (2 Timothy 3:15).

Many have health problems and are fighting illnesses because they did not apply the wisdom of eating healthy foods in the first place. Lots of people are battling diverse addictions simply because they did not practice abstinence. The reason why many parents are engaged in spiritual warfare to snatch their children from the Devil is because they did not heed the Bible's instruction to teach their children the ways of the Lord. If you do not teach your ward God's ways, they will go wayward. What you fail to do today will reap the consequence tomorrow. When you commit a blunder, you need to fight hard in order to get the plunder.

How to Take the Plunder After a Blunder

A blunder is a gross, stupid, foolish, or careless mistake. A mere mistake sometimes is inevitable, but a blunder is avoidable. You commit a blunder by acting carelessly, but you can get the plunder by praying seriously. To plunder is to take goods by force (as in a war), and Jesus talked about this in Matthew 11:12: *From the days of John the*

Baptist until now, the kingdom of heaven suffereth violence, and the violent take it by force.*

Preparing For a Battle

The second part of our passage teaches us that a king going to make war with another king must first of all sit down to evaluate his numerical strength. This is true before one engages in a battle or spiritual warfare too. It's very important to consider one's numerical strength. If the battle is too strong for you, do not hesitate to solicit the help of other believers in prayers. For one shall put a thousand to a flight, and two shall chase ten thousand.

> *Again I say unto you, That if two of you shall agree on earth as touching anything that they shall ask, it shall be done for them of my Father which is in heaven* (Matthew 18:19).

You do not need everybody; you simply need somebody who can stand in agreement with you. If the effectual, fervent prayer of one righteous man avails much, then the prayers of two or more righteous men will definitely prevail. In preparing for battle, spiritual or inner strength should also be evaluated apart from numerical strength. You put on the whole armor of God, and you ask the Lord to teach your hands for war and your fingers for battle.

> *You do not need everybody; you simply need somebody who can stand in agreement with you.*

> *Who goeth a warfare any time at his own charges?* (1 Corinthians 9:7a).

Dividing the Spoils

After sitting down to prepare for the battle first, then you go into the battle. In the attack or assault stage, there is also something you need to do first. That is, you bind the strong man.

> *Or else how can one enter into a strong man's house, and spoil his goods, except he **first bind the strong man?** And then he will spoil his house* (Matthew 12:29, emphasis mine).

> *When a strong man armed keepeth his palace, his goods are in peace. But when a stronger than he shall come upon him and overcome him, he taketh from him all his armour wherein he trusteth, and divideth his spoils* (Luke 11:21-22).

Who is the strong man? It is the Devil! Here Jesus described Satan as a strong man who has constructed a palace and filled it to capacity with goods and guarding it jealously. The question is: What kind of goods does the Devil have in there? Does he rightfully own any goods at all? For your information, they are all stolen goods; he stole them from you and me. He steals our peace, our health, our children, our finances, our businesses, our marriages, and more. The Devil is a thief.

> *The thief cometh not but for to steal, and to kill and to destroy: I am come that they might have life, and that they might have it more abundantly* (John 10:10).

Come Upon the Devil

Jesus went on to say that when one stronger than the Devil comes upon him, he over powers the Devil. Now, who is the one stronger than the Devil? It is you the believer, the born-again child of God, Spirit-filled, Holy Ghost-baptized, holy and tongue-talking person!

Maybe when I mentioned that the Devil is a strong man, fear went down your spine. Don't fear the Devil. You are stronger than him, because He that is in you is greater than he that is in the world. You are seated together with Christ in heavenly places far above all principalities and powers and dominion and every name that can be named in this world and the world to come. You have the whole armor of God: the belt of truth, the breastplate of righteousness, the shield of faith, helmet of salvation, and sword of the Spirit.

And hath raised us up together, and made us sit together in heavenly places in Christ Jesus (Ephesians 2:6).

You are a sorry example of kingdom power and authority if you fear witches and wizards. It is below your spiritual dignity as an anointed child of the Anointed One. Witches and wizards are believed to do astral travel, but we do not do that. We are already seated with Christ in heavenly places. When they fly, the furthest and highest they can get to is under our feet. Jesus talked about this in Luke 10:19: *Behold, I give unto you power to tread on serpents and scorpions, and over all the power of the enemy: and nothing shall by any means hurt you.*

Serpents bite with the mouth which is on the head. Scorpions sting with their tails. It means we have power over Satan himself who is the head to the last or least demon represented by the tail.

The fact that you are stronger than the Devil does not mean you should relax. You need to be on the offensive and aggressive. Remember that the best way to defend is to attack. You come upon him in the name of Jesus, by the power of the Holy Ghost, and with all the weapons you have at your disposal.

Come upon the Devil or run after him just like David ran after the lion and the bear that took a lamb from his flock. Be in haste like David who ran toward the Philistine army. Pursue the Devil like he pursued the Amalekites and recovered.

I hear the Spirit of the Lord say, "come upon the Devil, run after him, pursue him, and you will overcome, overpower, overtake, and without fail recover all." Remember that the thief (the Devil) is your target, so do not waste your missiles. You are a loaded gun; fire your missiles on target!

> *I therefore so run, not as uncertainly; so fight I, not as one that beateth the air* (1 Corinthians 9:26).

Overcome Him

If you are a boxing fan, you are familiar with the statement "the fight was fixed." The outcome of our fight with the Devil is known beforehand, because Jesus has already defeated him on the cross. We simply enter into the fight by enforcing our victory and enforcing his defeat! He is a defeated foe! He and his minions may be millions, but we still have dominion! He and his cohorts may be a host, but our God is the God of hosts!

> *And having spoiled principalities and powers, he made a shew of them openly, triumphing over them in it* (Colossians 2:15).

Take All the Weapons He Trusts from Him

After rendering the Devil ineffective and inoperative, it is imperative to take from him all the weapons he trusts. It may shock you to know that the weapons Satan trusts are your own weaknesses, prayerlessness, laziness, sin, doubts, and fear. He uses them to work against you by staging a comeback or counter-attacking. That is why Paul gives the admonition to stand ready to fight again, after having done all (Ephesians 6:13).

You may ask, "Why don't we strip the Devil of his armor before we come against him?" Usually, we relax after a major victory, and that is the moment Satan strikes back. He tempted Jesus after His successful long fast (Matthew 4:4). Immediately, when the Philistines heard that David had been anointed king over Israel, they met him to wage war against him (2 Samuel 5:17). New levels, new devils! New heights, new fights! New opportunities, new oppositions! New cups, new traps! New trophies, new catastrophes! The list goes on and on.

Divide the Spoils

Finally, you divide the spoils. This is where you take back all that the enemy stole from you. You turn over every stone and look under every rock. Here the Devil will definitely try to negotiate with you and say you can take this but not that. You need the resilience and the uncompromising attitude of Moses as when Pharaoh tried to strike a deal with him in his move to evacuate the people of Israel from Egypt.

> *New levels, new devils! New heights, new fights! New opportunities, new oppositions! New cups, new traps! New trophies, new catastrophes! The list goes on and on.*

The deal Pharaoh offered was that they could go with the people, including their little ones, and serve the Lord, but they had to leave behind the flocks and herds.

> *Our cattle also shall go with us; there shall not an hoof be left behind; for thereof must we take to serve the Lord our God; and we know not with what we must serve the LORD, until we come thither* (Exodus 10:26).

A hoof is a delicate part of an animal which is made of dead cells. Like Moses, we should not leave the smallest and most insignificant thing in the hands of the Devil. Take back all that he has stolen from you! Take the plunder!

> *Men do not despise a thief, if he steal to satisfy his soul when he is hungry. But if he be found, he shall restore sevenfold; he shall give all the substance of his house* (Proverbs 6:30-31).

CHAPTER FOUR

Seek the Main Thing, Get the Remaining, and Maintain the Main Thing

In Matthew chapter 6:33, we read the words of Jesus: *But seek ye first the Kingdom of God and his righteousness; and all these things shall be added unto you.*

There is no verse of Scripture that emphasizes prioritizing well in life like this one. However, take the word *first* out, and the verse loses its value and the real meaning Jesus wanted to communicate. Some Scriptures, if you remove just a word, as small a word as it may be, you take away the real meaning of the verse. In fact, there are some verses you cannot even paraphrase or rephrase. No wonder the Bible warns us not to take from or add to Scripture.

In the above text, the Lord Jesus was very emphatic and tells us without ambiguity what our ambition should be: to seek **first** His kingdom and His righteousness. It must be second to none. Jesus was in effect saying, seek the main thing, get the remaining and then maintain the main thing. The main thing to seek is the kingdom of God. To seek the kingdom of God is to seek God and vice versa. God and His kingdom are inseparable just like God and love. He is the King in the place of dominion.

Businesses have different kinds of promotional strategies aimed at boosting sales and revenue. One such strategy is to have people buy an item and receive a giveaway (gift), and it best explains this very popular and all-important piece of Scripture. For example, you may come across a promotion something like one of these: for every 50 purchases receive 5 iTunes gift cards, buy a car and get a free bicycle, buy a mobile phone and get a free sim card with credits, etc.

Now you realize that the main item you are supposed to buy is of superior value than the gift or prize being offered. It's never the opposite in any such promotional offer. In the same way, you can in nowise compare *all these things* and the value of the kingdom of God. In one of His parables, Jesus described the kingdom as a hidden treasure and fine pearls.

> *Again, the kingdom of heaven is like unto TREASURE hid in a field, the which when a man hath found he hideth, and for joy thereof goeth and selleth all that he hath, and buyeth that field. Again, the kingdom of heaven is like unto a merchant man, seeking goodly PEARLS: Who, when he had found one pearl of great price, went and sold all that he had and bought it* (Matthew 13:44-46, emphasis mine).

You cannot have the giveaway without first buying the main item. You also cannot buy the main item without getting the giveaway. In the same vein, you cannot have blessings without first seeking the one who blesses. You cannot seek the one who blesses and not get His blessings. It is automatic. Seek first the kingdom of God and have all things added unto you. Such blessing is authentic. Trying to seek the blessings without first seeking the one who blesses leads to bitter lessons. Seeking miracles without seeking first the worker of miracles creates a mirage. You are next in line for a miracle because you have not sidelined God and His kingdom!

The blessing of the Lord, it maketh rich, and he addeth no sorrow with it (Proverbs 10:22).

Jesus said when we seek first His kingdom, all other things shall be added unto us. Obviously, all "these things" refer to what to eat, what to drink and what to wear. We know this because Jesus was encouraging His disciples not to be bothered by such concerns in the previous verses. Let's take a look at it.

Therefore I say unto you, take no thought for your life, what ye shall eat, or what ye shall drink; nor yet for your body, what ye shall put on. Is not the life more than meat, and the body than raiment? Behold the fowls of the air: for they sow not, neither do they reap, nor gather into barns; yet your heavenly Father feedeth them. Are ye not much better than they? Which of you by taking thought can add one cubit unto his stature? And why take ye thought for raiment? Consider the lilies of the field, how they grow; they toil not, neither do they spin: and yet I say unto you, that even Solomon in all his glory was not arrayed like one of these. Wherefore, if God so clothe the grass of the field, which today is and tomorrow is cast into the oven, shall he not much more clothe you, O ye of little faith? Therefore take no thought, saying, What shall we eat? Or, what shall we drink? Or, wherewithal shall we be clothed? (For after all these things do the Gentiles seek:) for your heavenly Father knoweth that ye have need of all these things.

But seek ye first the kingdom of God, and his righteousness; and all these things shall be added unto you (Matthew 6:25-33).

We see the phrase *all these things* in verses 32 and 33. It refers to the food, drink, and clothing Jesus was telling them not to be bothered with in the preceding verses. In fact, anything we seek apart from God is a thing. Food, clothes, promotion, success, favor, job, marriage, career, money, or house are all things. All these countless things that we chase in life can be summed up as what we eat, drink, and put on our bodies.

In verse 32, Jesus pointed out that the Gentiles seek after material things. By Gentiles, Jesus meant people who do not know God or are without God in this world. Obviously, they sideline God and seek after material things. The believer, on the other hand, ought to walk in line with the Word, seeking God and His kingdom first.

Today, everyone (the believer and the unbeliever alike) seems to be preoccupied with these kinds of concerns that lead to questions like: What will I eat? How will I pay my bills? How will I have a happy marriage? How will I have a successful career?

There is no denying these needs are necessities. But the fact is that these things we desperately seek after, run after, fight over, chase, scramble for, covet and do all that is humanly possible to grab (not taking into consideration whether or not our means please God) are supposed to be our rewards, benefits, bonuses, top-ups, add-ons, and additions after we have diligently sought God's kingdom first. They accompany seeking the Lord and His kingdom first.

Jesus asked an important question in verse 25: *Is not the life more than meat and the body than raiment?* The answer is obviously yes! Life is more important than food and the body more important than clothing. How the organs in your body function to keep you alive is a very complex exercise. What Jesus was saying in effect is that if I can keep your heart beating and blood flowing in your system, then

I can put food on your table and clothing on your body! That is the deep revelation we should grasp!

Be Diligent in Seeking God and His Kingdom

Without faith it is impossible to please him for he that cometh to God must believe that he is, and that he is a rewarder of them that diligently seek him (Hebrews 11:6).

The above verse teaches that you must not just be a seeker of God and His kingdom but a diligent seeker. Do not be lackadaisical; be radical. Do not relax; pay the price. Listen, if you seek God with great tenacity, He will bless you in the city, out of the city, in the field, and everywhere you find yourself! The blessings of God will come upon you and overtake you! When you seek God first with diligence, then you can shout it without a shadow of doubt that goodness and mercy shall follow you all the days of your life.

Surely goodness and mercy shall follow me all the days of my life and I will dwell in the house of the Lord for ever (Psalm 23:6).

Surely is not a probability but a certainty. David was sure and, therefore, could shout it without a shadow of a doubt that goodness and mercy were going to follow him because he was a God chaser. This was the man the Bible said was after God's own heart. David longed after and chased God. If we pursue or chase after God, He will command His blessings to chase or follow us. If we neglect, sideline, and by-pass God and His kingdom and chase after His blessings, it will be a mirage. Goodness and mercy must not be in front of us for us to do the chasing; they must be behind to do the chasing. Stop chasing blessings and chase the Blesser.

Twin Sisters

Goodness and mercy are two different things. In fact, I call them twin sisters. Sister Goodness follows us when we faithfully obey the commands of God. But because we are still in this body and are bound to make mistakes and inevitably miss the mark sometimes, because we have shortfalls and shortcomings, Sister Mercy shows up when we do not deserve His goodness.

The all-knowing God knows the shortfalls of His people; this is why when He arises upon His church, the first thing He does is to have mercy.

> *Thou shalt arise, and have mercy upon Zion: for the time to favor her, yea, the set time is come* (Psalm 102:13).

Be Rooted, Grounded and Unmovable in the Kingdom

> *...and I will dwell in the house of the Lord forever* (Psalm 23:6b).

What David is saying in the above verse is that when he is blessed by God, he will still dwell in the house of the Lord. He will continue to be in the kingdom and not forget Jerusalem. Some Christians stop serving God when what they are expecting from the Lord is not forthcoming. Ironically, some also allow what they have been blessed with to take them out of God's presence. More often than not, people come into the Lord broke, broken, ugly, sick, jobless, and childless. When God starts to bless them and make their lives beautiful, before long, they are nowhere to be found in the church. The brother who once upon a time had no job now gives excuse and says "my job" when asked why he is not in church anymore. A once single and just married Christian also gives the spouse as an excuse for being absent from church meetings. They simply allow their blessings to take the place of God, and eventually this practice takes them out of fellowship.

God's blessings are never intended to make us backslidden, lukewarm, or lackadaisical but to encourage us to serve Him better. They are tools and vehicles to enhance our service and commitment to God. They are intended to increase our faith to receive more and even greater blessings from God. The Bible gives us this warning! *If riches increase, set not your heart upon them* (Psalm 62:10b).

Beware Lest the Things You Own Come to Own You

Hardly will a thing outside your environment take the place of God. It is always the things in our domain; the things we call our own that try to own us. Be careful you do not let a thing be your king!

In Exodus 32:1-4, the children of Israel put intense pressure on Aaron to make gods for them. Eventually, Aaron succumbed, and they removed the golden earrings they carried in their ears, and he fashioned them into a golden image.

> *And when the people saw that Moses delayed to come down out of the mount, the people gathered themselves together unto Aaron, and said unto him, Up, make us gods, which shall go before us; for as for this Moses, the man that brought us up out of the land of Egypt, we wot not what is become of him.*
>
> *And Aaron said unto them, Break off the golden earrings which are in the ears of your wives, of your sons and of your daughters and bring them unto me. And all the people brake off the golden earrings which were in their ears, and brought*

> *them unto Aaron. And he received them at their hand, and fashioned it with a graving tool, after he had made it a molten calf: and they said, These be thy gods, O Israel, which brought thee out of the land of Egypt.*

Now these ungrateful children of Israel soon forgot the God who carried them from Egypt, and now they worshipped a god made from earrings they wore in their ears. They forgot the God who parted the Red Sea and worshipped earrings formed into the shape of a calf. Meanwhile, God explicitly told them in the twentieth chapter of Exodus not to have any other gods besides Him, not to make any graven image, and not to bow down to them or serve them.

Today, our attitudes towards the goodness and mercies of God are no different from the people of Israel. We let what we carried from the market carry us away from God. We easily forget how far God has brought us, and we allow what we bought to make us forget we were bought with a price.

Let me ask you a question by paraphrasing the words of the apostle Paul in 1 Corinthians 4:7: *What do you have that you did not receive and if you did receive it, why do you treat and worship it as though it is your god?* It grieves the heart of God when we allow material prosperity to steal our heart and make us backslide. Do not let your career or possessions be a barrier between you and your God.

> *But thou shalt remember the LORD thy God: for it is he that giveth thee power to get wealth, that he may establish his covenant which he sware unto thy fathers, as it is this day* (Deuteronomy 8:18).

We should not quote the above Scripture only to remind ourselves to tithe but also remind us to hold unto the Lord tight. We should remember and endeavor to serve the Lord all the days of our lives.

God Has Not Finished With You Yet

The Bible tells us in Philippians 1:6 that the good things God begins to do in (or to, with, through) our lives, He will complete them. It grieves God when we walk away from Him in the beginning of His dealings with us. He wants us to allow Him to continue till He completes what He has started.

> *The man began to prosper, and continued prospering until he became very prosperous* (Genesis 26:13 NKJV).

This text is talking about Isaac when he sowed in a barren land, and God caused him to be fruitful amidst great opposition from the people of Gerar. When he began to prosper, he did not quit; he stayed focused until he became very prosperous. When you become prosperous, it's for your own consumption; but when you become very prosperous, you become a blessing to others. When your cup is full, it's for your own satisfaction; but when it begins to run over, you impact and bless others. You are blessed now, but allow God to bless you more until you become a blessing. That's the covenant promise.

When your cup is full, it's for your own satisfaction; but when it begins to run over, you impact and bless others.

The Bible speaks of King Uzziah who was enthroned as a king at the young age of sixteen. This young man ruled and became prosperous by seeking the Lord continually.

> *And he sought God in the days of Zechariah who had understanding in the visions of God: and as long as he sought the Lord, God made him to prosper* (2 Chronicles 26:5).

I like the phrase *as long as he sought the Lord, God made him to prosper*. "As long as" suggests continuity, diligence, persistence, and perseverance. As he diligently sought the Lord constantly, his prosperity continued. For some people, as soon as God prospers them, they become content and complacent.

Isaac became very prosperous, and King Uzziah had a lasting prosperity all as a result of continuity in their relationship with God. When we seek God and His kingdom first, He would say, "let the children first be filled."

CHAPTER FIVE

Priorities, Blessings and Crumbs

I have talked about seeking first the kingdom of God and having all things added unto you. It is one of the aspects of our Christian life that is often emphasized. However, what we fail to realize is that God also is a God of priority. In that one area, He sets priorities when it comes to releasing His blessings.

In the first place, I want to point out one scriptural truth. The Bible categorizes all humans into two groups: the children of God and the children of the Devil. This is a truth unbelievers just cannot accept. They are quick to reiterate, "But we are all God's children."

Sorry, that's a big No! To become God's child, you must be born again; till then, you remain His creation. A product is not a son or daughter of its manufacturer. God is your Creator, but you do not become His child until you become born again.

> *But as many as received him, to them gave he power to become the sons of God; even to them that believe on his name* (John 1:12).
>
> *In this the children of God are manifest, and the children of the devil…* (1 John 3:10a).

In the second Scripture, John draws a clear line of distinction in the sand.

Paul looked at Bar-jesus, eyeball to eyeball, and said *thou child of the devil* (Acts 13:10). Jesus interacted with the Jews who claimed

Abraham and God to be their fathers. Without apology, Jesus replied to them that their father was the Devil (John 8:44). Take note that Paul and Jesus were not talking to inanimate things; they were talking to humans.

Being a child of the Devil does not mean Satan created or gave birth to them. The word *father* used here implies "a source; a person who has originated or established something." By refusing to put their faith in God, they become the Devil's children, because he is their source of inspiration, their lying tendencies, their wickedness, and other sinful tendencies.

The next truth I want to establish is that, between the child of God and the unbeliever, God's priority is always the former when it comes to releasing blessings, granting protection, giving provision and any other blessing you can think of. That is to say being born again comes with glorious privileges and advantages.

Birthright and Privileges

Among the Jews, birthright had significant spiritual blessings connected to it. It denotes special advantages and privileges belonging to the first-born son in the Jewish family. These included the honor of becoming the patriarch and the priest of the family after the death of the father, receiving a double portion of the paternal inheritance (Deuteronomy 21:15-17), inheriting every kind of judicial authority of the father (2 Chronicles 21:3), and much more.

By reason of our being born-again sons and daughters of God, we also have a precious birthright. Our birthright is our Christianity! We have been reborn into the family of God, and as such we have unsurpassed privileges and advantages. The enemy is aware of your privileges and advantages, so he will fight you. I pray you may never be like Reuben and Esau who forfeited the blessings and privileges associated with their birthrights.

The above mentioned individuals sinned. Reuben's sin is obvious, as he slept with his father's concubine (Genesis 35:22), but for Esau's sin, one may question the seriousness. The fact that the writer of the book of Hebrews likened him to a fornicator and a profane person (Hebrews 12:16) settles the argument. Those are strong words! The point is sin halts the flow of God's blessings into the life of the believer. We cannot expect God to shower us with His blessings when we live in continual disobedience and disregard of His Word.

> *Your iniquities have turned away these things, and your sins have withholden good things from you* (Jeremiah 5:25).

Scriptural promises on God's protection, healing, provision, His abiding presence, answered prayer, peace, victory over sin and Satan, and more are exclusive benefits of those who have committed their lives to the Lord Jesus Christ. How do we know that? Often, words and phrases like "beloved," "my son," "my people," "in Christ," "those that wait upon the Lord," "those that love Him," "if you abide in me and my Word abide in you" and the like are found in the same context of such scriptural promises. Below is an example:

> *If **my people**, which are **called by my name**, shall humble themselves, and pray, and seek my face, and turn from their wicked ways; then will I hear from heaven, and will forgive their sin, and will heal their land* (2 Chronicles 7:14, emphasis mine).

Concerning grace, there are different kinds. Peter mentioned in 1 Peter 5:10 that God is the God of all grace. He again said that God's grace varies or is manifold in 1 Peter 4:10. People who have not put their trust in God only enjoy the common, basic grace or the general grace of God. It is the grace that causes the sun to shine on the just and unjust alike and also the rain to fall on both (Matthew 5:45).

God loves both the sinner and the saint. However, He has a covenant relationship with His children and has given them exceeding great and precious promises (2 Peter 1:4). As a result, there are other levels of grace reserved for the saints. The believer comes first when it comes to blessings.

Children First

The story of the Syrophenician or the Canaanite woman reveals that not only do real blessings belong to children of God and crumbs for unbelievers, but this account also reveals God gives priority to the former.

> *And from thence he arose, and went into the borders of Tyre and Sidon, and entered into an house, and would have no man know it: but he could not be hid. For a certain woman whose young daughter had an unclean spirit, heard of him, and came and fell at his feet: The woman was a Greek, a Syrophenician by nation; and she besought him that he would cast forth the devil out of her daughter. But Jesus said unto her, let the children first be filled: for it is not meet to take the children's bread, and cast it unto dogs. And she answered and said unto him, yes, Lord, yet the dogs under the table eat of the children's crumbs. And he said unto her, For this saying, go thy way; the devil is gone out of thy daughter. And when she was come to her house, she found the devil gone out and her daughter laid upon the bed* (Mark 7:24-30).

The interaction of this woman with Jesus brings to the fore a powerful revelation regarding the dealings of God with His children and those who are not His. Jesus' statement, *let the children first be filled: for it is not right to take the children's bread and cast it unto dogs* points out that true blessings belong to the children of God, whereas the worldly deserve crumbs according to the woman's faith-filled statement: *yet the dogs under the table eat of the children's crumbs.* By children, Jesus meant the Jewish people to whom He was sent. By reason of the new birth, we have also become children and spiritual Israelites.

The woman was a Gentile, and she represents the worldly or unregenerate. In fact, "dogs" in the Scriptures metaphorically refer to unbelievers or backsliders.

> *For without are dogs, and sorcerers, and whoremongers, and murderers and idolaters and whosoever loveth and maketh a lie* (Revelation 22:15).

> *For it had been better for them not to have known the way of righteousness, than, after they have known it, to turn from the holy commandment delivered unto them. But it is happened unto them according to the true proverb, The dog is turned to his own vomit again: and the soul that was washed to her wallowing in the mire* (2 Peter 2:21-22).

The text in Revelation names "dogs" among the list of folks who will be outside the gates of heaven. They are not literal dogs to guard heaven's gates but people who lived sinful lifestyles on earth.

Besides real blessings going out to the children of God, they are also at the top of God's priority list. That explains the statement, *Let the children **first** be filled*. This is a too-good-to-be-true revelation for the believer. If you are a child of God, by God's grace you are in a position to receive the booty and the priority. Everyone who serves God is in line for a first serve. While believers take the plunder, unbelievers lurk in wait under the table to pick up the crumbs. Those who wait on God receive a weight of blessings, while those who do not want God get the wastes the former do not want or are willing to share. Praise God!

No wonder Jesus commanded the disciples to gather the crumbs and leftovers after feeding five thousand of His followers. Perhaps He knew they were for non-followers! One of the reasons Jesus is against wastage is that unbelievers can have it as a consolation package!

> *One of the reasons Jesus is against wastage is that unbelievers can have it as a consolation package!*

> *When they were filled, he said unto his disciples, Gather up the fragments that remain, that nothing be lost* (John 6:12).

Just like the woman who pleaded for crumbs, Esau also received a consolation blessing after his plea. Jacob, the new holder of the birthright had already received the real blessings which were irreversible and irrevocable. Esau was left with no option but to beg for a leftover blessing. Hear his plea here.

> *And when Esau heard the words of his father, he cried with a great and exceeding bitter cry, and said unto his father, Bless me, even me also, O my father . . . And Esau said unto his father, Hast thou but one blessing, my father? Bless me, even me also, O my father. And Esau lifted up his voice, and wept* (Genesis 27:34, 38).

Unbelievers beg God. Believers are not to beg but ask God. *Ask and it shall be given unto you,* the Bible says. In the parable of the widow and the wicked judge, the former literally begged the latter to grant her justice. That parable teaches us persistency in our asking but not to have a begging attitude in our approach to God. The woman begged the judge because he was wicked and callous. Our God is good, and His mercies endure forever. We beg wicked men, but as His children, we ask a kind God.

The gospel of John says those who have put their trust in Jesus have been given the right to be called the children of God (John 1:12 NIV). Jesus told the woman that it was not right for Him to take the children's bread and give it to her (Mark 7:28, NIV). Now, if something is not right, it's wrong or an error. In the book of Ecclesiastes, the preacher observed such an error.

> *There is an evil which I have seen under the sun, as an error which proceedeth from the ruler:*
>
> *Folly is set in great dignity and the rich sit in low place. I have seen servants upon horses, and princes walking as servants upon the earth* (Ecclesiastes 10:5-7).

The preacher saw this error in the world by observation. Now, let us get into the Word to see what is right by revelation.

A Mind Blowing Revelation

In Galatians 6:10, Paul admonished the Galatian Christians to do good to all men, especially fellow Christians. *As we have therefore opportunity, let us do good unto all men, especially unto them who are of the household of faith.*

One thing I want you to bear in mind is that God never tells you to do something He Himself would do otherwise. He tells us to do what He does, love what He loves, and hate what He hates.

Because He does good to all men irrespective of whether they are His children or not, He wants us to follow suit as His followers. However, the second part of the verse emphasizes that we should give priority to fellow brethren in the faith. That means if you hear of an employment opportunity, ideally, you should inform a fellow Christian or, better still, let it be announced in the church. If nobody in the church is interested, then you can let an unbelieving friend grasp that opportunity.

That is what God does. The word *especially* means "in a special manner, chiefly, particularly, peculiarly, in an uncommon degree." God is good to all, but He gives priority to His children in the household of faith. He gives them uncommon favor, uncommon blessings, and uncommon protection.

The next Scripture that buttresses this revelation is 1Timothy 5:8. Like our Scripture in Galatians, this Scripture speaks to us regarding God's serious intentions to bless the believer abundantly.

> *But if any provide not for his own, and specially for those of his own house, he hath denied the faith and is worse than an infidel* (1Timothy 5:8).

This Scripture infers that we ought to provide for our own and those who are related, associated, and connected to our lives. They could be friends, relatives, and acquaintances. Nevertheless, in providing for our own, we must give preference to those in our own house, our nuclear family. We must make sure our nuclear family is cared and catered for, before we extend our hands to our extended families. It is improper to bypass the former to bless the latter. The saying "charity begins at home" rightly applies here.

Again, what is the revelation? The revelation is that God provides for His own creation (every individual, including birds, animals, and every living thing), but He gives preference and abundance to those in His own House. He first satisfies the members of His own body, members of His own family.

Let me give you one last Scripture in regards to this. It is in the form of a question.

> *He that spared not his own Son, but delivered him up for us all, how shall he not with him also freely give us all things?* (Romans 8:32).

The obvious answer is that He will freely, abundantly, and willingly give us all things. If someone is able to give you his best, he can easily give you the rest. If you refuse his best, he will deny you the rest, as in the case of those who have rejected His so great salvation.

Jesus is God's best gift to mankind. How do we know that? Jesus, the Son, is mentioned in the same context among the best, biggest, and greatest of all in the greatest text of all, John 3:16.

> *For God so love the world, that he gave his only begotten Son that whosoever believeth in him should not perish but have everlasting life.*

- God – the biggest and greatest of all
- Love – the greatest of all
- Son – the best gift of all
- Belief – the most important thing of all in one's life
- Everlasting life – the greatest gain of all

I see God freely give you all things! You shall not want if you have made the Lord your Shepherd! Nothing good shall He withhold from those who put their trust in Him! He shall meet you at the point of your needs! All His promises to you are yes and amen!

Beloved do not be envious when you see the prosperity of the wicked. The Devil may inspire them to use corrupt ways and means to get rich hastily, but their end is bleak and disastrous. They may build without the Lord but in the end, it will not stand. The end of the righteous is peace!

Let not thy heart envy sinners: but be thou in the fear of the Lord all the day long. For surely, there is an end; and thine expectation shall not be cut off (Proverbs 23:17-18).

To be in the fear of the Lord is to walk in the ways of the Lord. Say no to the ways of the world and go the Word's or God's ways.

CHAPTER SIX

The World's Ways vs. The Word's Ways

There are basically two kingdoms in this life, namely: the kingdom of God and the kingdom of the Devil. These two kingdoms are diametrically opposed and mutually exclusive to each other. Each has its own principles, beliefs, philosophies, ideologies, mindsets, and so on. The principles and the ways of doing things in the kingdom of God are outlined in the Bible. I call it the "Word's Ways." The principles and the ways of doing things in the kingdom of darkness, on the other hand, are evidenced in the world. I call it the "World's Ways."

The Word's ways are what the Word prescribes, and the world's ways are what the world describes as good. The world's ways are vile, wide, wild, weird, and full of the Devil's lies and wiles, while the Word's ways are good, perfect, and the acceptable will of God.

Because we live in this world, there is a threat and strong temptation to live our lives according to the standards of the world. The Bible however cautions us against conforming to this world and admonishes us to transform to biblical standards.

> *And be not conformed to this world: but be ye transformed by the renewing of your mind, that ye may prove what is that good, and acceptable, and perfect, will of God* (Romans 12:2).

As believers, we are to go the Word's way and not the world's way, so we can make headway in every area of life. In order to go the Word's way with a full commitment, the believer must take time to get away from the world, be in the Word, and let the Word be in him richly. The believer must leave the world's way, cleave to the Word's way and live it. The Christian must stop practicing the ways of the world, step with both feet into the ways of the Word, and start walking in them.

> *Enter not into the path of the wicked, and go not in the way of evil men. Avoid it, pass not by it, turn from it, and pass away* (Proverbs 4:14-15).

Unfortunately, the world's ways have crept into Christendom in a variety of ways. Christians consciously or unconsciously apply the principles of the world instead of the principles outlined in God's Word. It does not matter how sweet they sound, appealing they seem, or attractively they are packaged, the believer should not buy them. They may be applicable and in a worldly sense successful, but they are not acceptable to God. They may be facts but short of absolute truths.

> *As believers, we are to go the Word's way and not the world's way, so we can make headway in every area of life.*

The child of God cannot beat or compete with unbelievers when he chooses to walk in their ways, because they have expertise and a great deal of experience in the way they do things. It is familiar territory or "home ground" for them. The only thing worth emulating from the world is the seriousness, passion, and tenacity with which they go about what they believe in. While the children of the kingdom of light are rather lackadaisical in their attitude, the children of the world are radical.

> *...for the children of this world are in their generation wiser than the children of light* (Luke 16:8b).

Below are some of the sayings which reveal the principles, mindset, and philosophies of the world which contrast what the Word of God teaches.

Philosophy # 1

The World: **Seeing Before Believing**

The Word: **Believing Before Seeing**

The world emphasizes that before you believe, you must see first. The Bible teaches the opposite; believe before you see. The story of doubting Thomas perfectly illustrates these two opposing principles or philosophies.

> *But Thomas, one of the twelve, called Didymus, was not with them when Jesus came. The other disciples therefore said unto him, We have seen the Lord. But he said unto them, Except I shall see in His hands the print of the nails, and put my finger into the print of the nails and thrust my hand into his side, I will not believe. And after eight days again his disciples were within, and Thomas with them: then came Jesus, the doors being shut, and stood in the midst and said, Peace be unto you. Then saith he unto Thomas, Reach hither thy finger and behold my hands: and reach hither thy hand, and thrust it into my side: and be not faithless, but believing. And Thomas answered and said unto him, My Lord and my God. Jesus saith unto him, Thomas, because thou hast seen me, thou hast believed: blessed are they that have not seen, and yet have believed* (John 20:24-29).

Thomas doubted his friends outright when they told him they had seen the resurrected Jesus. He wanted to see Jesus with his very eyes before he could believe. In fact, in addition to seeing, he wanted to feel and touch His scars as well. Thomas was a heavyweight doubter who cannot be surpassed by anyone in the history of mankind.

After Jesus satisfied his curiosity and inquisitiveness, then Thomas believed. A vital lesson to learn is that Jesus neither condemned nor approved of his kind of believing, that is, seeing before believing. Instead, He approved and highly recommended believing before seeing.

> *Jesus saith unto him, Thomas, because thou hast seen me, thou hast believed: blessed are they that have not seen, and yet have believed* (John 20:29).

Seeing before believing is a principle of the world. The world insists on seeing before they have faith. No wonder many people in the world find it difficult to believe in a Jesus they cannot physically see. Christianity is about believing without even seeing. We believe in Jesus, heaven, hell, and the like though we are yet to see them physically. We walk by faith not by sight. Faith is a sixth sense the Christian has, and he sees the invisible, the intangible, and the impossible with it. The unbeliever, on the other hand, only relies on the sense of sight.

The disciples of Jesus had the privilege of seeing Him, walking with Him, and eating with Him. For them, having faith in Jesus was not a big deal compared to us who see Him not and yet believe. When Jesus said blessed are those who have not seen and yet have believed, He was referring to present-day believers. Never wish you lived in the time Jesus was physically present on earth. He calls you blessed. In fact, your faith or Christianity is not inferior to that of the apostles who saw Jesus, walked with Him, and talked with Him.

> *Simon Peter, a servant and an apostle of Jesus Christ, to them that have obtained like precious faith with us, through the righteousness of God and our Savior Jesus Christ* (2 Peter 1:1).

Sometimes, God wants us to see not with physical eyes like the world sees, but with the eye of our heart. I pray you walk in faith and not by sight and that you will never insist on seeing before you believe but rather resist such tendency.

Philosophy # 2

The World: **Save and You Will Increase**

The Word: **Give and You Will Increase**

The world believes and encourages that one needs to save money in order to be rich or have financial increase. On the contrary, the Bible teaches that, in order to have financial increase, you need to give tithes, offerings, first fruits, and sow faith seed. Therefore, while the believer thinks in terms of how much he can give (selflessness), the unbeliever thinks in terms of how much he can get (self-centeredness). Saving in itself is not wrong. Too much emphasis on it at the expense of sowing in the kingdom of God, giving to support the work of God and people in need makes it wrong.

> *There is that scattereth, and yet increaseth: and there is that withholdeth more than is meet, but it tendeth to poverty* (Proverbs 11:24).

The Bible is quite clear; the verse is self-explanatory. The one who scatters experiences increase, but the one who hoards for himself ends up in poverty. The one who empties his hand ends up having to the full, but the one who withholds ends up empty. What a paradox!

To scatter is to cause a mass or aggregate to separate and go in different directions. It also means to throw about in different directions. When a cup of glass falls from your hands to the ground, it will break into many small particles and fall in different directions. That is an illustration of scattering.

God wants us to scatter our finances. This means we should do more than one kind of giving. The different directions our giving should take include: tithe, offering, alms, and more. We do not have to do one or some and leave others undone. When our finances go toward different kinds of giving, we shall undoubtedly have increase. In almost every verse on giving, there is a command and a promise attached, making the Word of God a two-edged sword indeed. Let's look at a few examples.

> ***Give,*** *and it shall be **given unto you**, good measure, pressed down, shaken together, running over, shall men **give into your bosom*** (Luke 6:38, emphasis mine).
>
> ***Honour*** *the Lord with thy substance, and with the first fruits of all thine increase: **so shall thy barns be filled with plenty, and thy presses shall burst out with new wine*** (Proverbs 3:9, 10, emphasis mine).
>
> ***Cast*** *thy bread upon the waters: for thou shall **find it** after many days* (Ecclesiastes 11:1, emphasis mine).

As you can see, the first parts of these verses are commands. That tells us giving is not optional. The second parts also contain promises to receive back in abundance. The Philippian church saw this revelation. That is why they communicated to Paul about giving and receiving. Your harvest will always be better and bigger than your seed, especially when the soil is good. Be a giver and let the Lord prosper you.

Philosophy # 3

The World: **The End Justifies the Means**
The Word: **The Means is as Important as the End**

"The end justifies the means" is a popular saying of the world to justify their ungodly and dubious ways and means of doing things. Due to this mindset, unbelievers use fair and foul means to amass wealth, get success, power, fame, and the like. They do not consider whether or not God approves of their pragmatic means as long as it leads to their desired results or destination.

For instance, a person who wants to get to the top does not care if they kill, cheat, slander, backbite, or blackmail others to get there. People who want to get wealth overnight resort to gambling, embezzlement, cheating, stealing and all sorts of crooked and ungodly ways.

A faithful man shall abound with blessings: but he that maketh haste to be rich shall not be innocent (Proverbs 28:20).

If you skip biblical principles such as tithing, giving offerings, and helping the poor in order to be rich quick, you shall not be innocent, though you may gain worldly wealth. Anything you gain by taking a worldly short-cut will be short-lived. Anything done or gained God's way will always outlive you. The end justifies the means is not an absolute truth. The natural man is only interested in final results, but God takes a critical look at the means right to the end, to mark your actions as right or wrong. God's marking structure differs from man's.

> *Anything you gain by taking a worldly short-cut will be short-lived.*

Life can be likened to solving a mathematical problem; every good examiner is interested in the formula and the steps you used to arrive at your final answer, but not just the latter. He looks at every step and gives marks. If your formula is right, and you went through the right steps, your answer is likely to be right. If your formula is wrong or some steps are skipped, you may get a failed mark even though your final answer may be correct. The end does not always justify the means; the means is as important as the end in the sight of God.

God is all-knowing and also weighs actions.

> *Talk no more so exceeding proudly: let not arrogancy come out of your mouth: for the Lord is a God of knowledge, and by him actions are weighed* (1 Samuel 2:3).

Philosophy # 4

The World: **Vengeance and Retaliation**

The Word: **Forgiveness and Reconciliation**

Being at loggerheads and not being on speaking terms are ways of the world. The following expressions are widely used by the worldly: "you do me, I do you," "tit for tat," "eye for eye and tooth for tooth." It is a principle of the world that encourages paying one back in one's own coin.

While the world promotes and condones vengeance and retaliation, the Bible condemns it and promotes forgiveness and reconciliation. The believer is required to forgive and leave vengeance to God. He or she is admonished to try as much as possible to live peacefully with everyone.

> *Recompense to no man evil for evil. Provide things honest in the sight of all men. If it be possible, as much as lieth in you, live peaceably with all men. Dearly beloved, avenge not yourselves, but rather give place unto wrath: for it is written, Vengeance is mine; I will repay saith the Lord. Therefore if thine enemy hunger, feed him; if he thirst, give him drink: for in so doing, thou shalt heap coals of fire on his head. Be not overcome of evil but overcome evil with good* (Romans 12:17-21).

You make yourself God by usurping His authority. From the passage above, one of the things God claims sole ownership of is vengeance. Anything that God says is His, we dare not venture to claim, lest we play god. He says vengeance is mine, I will repay!

When you hurt someone, it is easy to say "sorry," but when you get hurt by someone, it is difficult to say "it's alright" when you know you are right. Our natural reaction to hurts and offences is to take revenge and retaliate. However, the superior life in the Spirit does not permit that. God admonishes us to forgive.

*Forgive us our **debts** as we forgive **our debtors*** (Matthew 6:12 NIV).

This Scripture is an excerpt from the Lord's Prayer, and it reveals that except we forgive those who offend us, God will not forgive us. Forgiving others is one of the prerequisites for receiving forgiveness of our own sins from the Lord. Since you and I need forgiveness from the Lord, it makes it imperative on our part to pardon people all the time. Pardoning people who hurt and offend us is very important. Leaving revenge or vengeance in the hands of God is also required of us. Peter added his voice to this command. *Not rendering evil for evil or railing for railing: but contrariwise blessing: knowing that ye are thereunto called, that ye should inherit a blessing* (1 Peter 3:9).

If you say these are difficult things to do, then how about the things you are supposed to do next; that is, blessing, feeding, loving, and praying for the people who have wronged you. You can now exclaim that Christianity is difficult!

If thine enemy be hungry, give him bread to eat: and if he be thirsty, give him water to drink: For thou shall heap coals of fire upon his head, and the LORD shall reward thee (Proverbs 25:21, 22).

Philosophy # 5

The World: **Practice What is Popular**

The Word: **Practice What is Proper**

The word *popular* refers to a prevailing practice, custom, fashion, or style of general appeal and wide usage among people. Another word often used to describe popular is *fad*. It is any form of behavior that develops among a large population, and it's collectively followed with enthusiasm momentarily. It could also be in the area of language usage, and even food.

Sometimes a fad or a popular phenomenon is called a "craze." That word *craze* must sound a warning to the believer not to follow what is popular because it is improper according to the standard of God's Word. That is to say, it is craziness to neglect the Word and follow the world.

The world changes rapidly. Things appear from nowhere and vanish into thin air in no time. Clichés come and go. The world believes and practices what is popular and what is in vogue. Everybody does what everybody is doing, everybody says what everybody is saying, and everybody wears what everybody is wearing. The Word, on the other hand, insists that we do what is proper. Our passion should be to please God.

Today, it is popular for women to dress indecently and be half naked. It is an eyesore on our streets and on television. Unfortunately, many of our Christian sisters do not heed the Bible's call to dress modestly. They dress indecently and weird just like the world.

> *And behold, there met him a woman with the attire of an harlot, and subtil of heart* (Proverbs 7:10).

When you see a policeman in uniform, you need not be told who he is because his uniform makes it clear. Uniforms inform. Sister in Christ, by reason of how you dress, do people identify you as a harlot or a Christian? Ladies, we are tired of the "attire of a harlot" many of you wear to church; so please try to dress well! Preachers do not want to look at your chest when laying hands on you to pray for you. When parts of your bodies are exposed, you become a stumbling block to your male counterparts in church because they are unable to concentrate. In fact, men cannot "watch" and pray when you fall under the power. While you are going down, your undies are peeping out and going up. If you dress decently, no cloth will be needed to cover you when you fall under the power. You are not changed because of the way you dress, but if you are really changed, you will change the way you dress to please God.

> *You are not changed because of the way you dress, but if you are really changed, you will change the way you dress to please God.*

In like manner also, that women adorn themselves in modest apparel (1Timothy 2:9a).

In today's world, sex before marriage is popular. Men demand it from their wives-to-be under the pretext that they need to test before they commit to entering into marriage. Interestingly, some women also offer it to their would-be-husbands under the deception that it will make the man love them more. Though it's not the biggest sin, as there is no measure of big or small sin, it is a serious sin with many repercussions. It must be avoided at all cost.

Divorce is rampant. Statistics both in the world and in the church are appalling and alarming. Christians and pastors alike are divorcing. Because it is popular, people turn to divorce even over trivial issues.

The Word requires the believer to do what is proper. The Christian is expected to stand up and stand out. God wants us to go against the flow. Do not sin because everybody is sinning.

Philosophy # 6

The World: **Calls Evil Good and Good Evil**

The Word: **Calls Good and Evil as They Are**

The world calls evil good and good evil. The Word, on the other hand, calls evil as it is and good as it is. When the Bible condemns something as sin, evil, or an abomination, the world tries to find a nice word, terminology, phrase or expression in an attempt to justify it.

> *Woe unto them that call evil good, and good evil; that put darkness for light, and light for darkness; that put bitter for sweet and sweet for bitter* (Isaiah 5:20).

"Woe" is not "oh" neither is it "wow!" It is not the sound of a dog's bark! It is a strong biblical word that introduces the wrath, fury, and judgment of God. When we insist on making our own judgments of what is right and wrong, we invite the judgment of God, and *woe* is the word that alerts us that He is coming with judgment, and we cannot stand it.

The Bible is not ambiguous at all concerning what is wrong and right. It lays out the way we should live, to do good and eschew evil. Society has placed evil in the place of good and vice versa. And the sad thing is that this mindset is creeping into the church. Things have been mixed up and turned upside down.

Today, sin is no longer called sin. It is called a mistake, and the sinner is also called a social deviant. A demon-possessed person is referred to as someone with a mental or psychological problem or disorder. Perversion is called an alternate lifestyle. Killing of unborn babies is called a choice. A harlot or a prostitute is called a commercial, sex worker, and adultery is an extramarital affair. Indecent dressing is fashion, and selfish ambition is passion. That old Bible word *fornication* is completely missing in our vocabulary, though it's a very common practice today. It is substituted with a much nicer phrase, pre-marital sex.

On top of calling evil good and good evil, the world also hates and despises good people and loves evil people (2 Timothy 3:3). They are also haters of God (Proverbs 8:36, Romans 1:30) and inventers of evil things (Romans 1:30). They use their corrupted wisdom and ingenuity to invent things that enhance and facilitate evil practices. Vibrators and other sex toys are such evil inventions.

The world applauds, adores, celebrates and hails evil-doers. By so doing, they encourage, stir and strengthen their hands to do more evil. The believer should love sinners but hate their sin. The believer should not be comfortable with sinners' sins but confront their sins.

CHAPTER SEVEN

Overcoming Addictions

One indicator of a person's value system is what he is addicted to. We tend to become addicted to the things we hold in high esteem. Webster's Dictionary defines addiction as "devoted to (someone or something), to give oneself habitually or compulsively." It is clear that addiction by its definition is not negative. It is the thing which one is addicted to that makes it negative or otherwise. The apostle Paul gives us a biblical clue as to how we can end up with a negative addiction in 1 Corinthians 6:12: All things are lawful unto me, but all things are not expedient: all things are lawful for me, but I will not be brought under the power of any.

What Paul is saying is that some things or activities can be lawful or permissible but not expedient, necessary, suitable, proper or appropriate. When we engage, indulge, or participate in them, they have the potency to bring us under their power. In other words, they will get us addicted to them. What then is addiction?

Having made that clarity, I am going to deal with only bad or negative addictions in this chapter and treat holy addictions in the next chapter. An aspect of arithmetic which deals with adding numbers is called addition. Addition and addiction sound similar, and the two words have something in common in terms of meaning. In my own words, I define negative addiction as adding up a particular sin. To better understand what I mean, consider this verse in Isaiah.

> *Woe to the rebellious children, saith the Lord that take counsel, but not of me; and that cover with a covering, but not of my spirit, that they may* **add sin to sin** (Isaiah 30:1, emphasis mine).

When you keep repeating one particular sin over and over and lack the power to stop, you are addicted. As an addict, that particular sin becomes a habit. Addictive habits can either be a secret sin or not. It may begin as a secret sin and come into the open when it gets into the addiction stage.

Signs of Addiction

You are addicted:
- If a particular sin so easily entangles you.
- When you are brought under the control of a particular sin.
- If the good you want to do, you are not able to do; but the evil you do not want to do is what you do.
- When you waste money, time, and energy on a particular sin.
- When you become a slave to a particular sin.

The Process of Addiction

A person who is addicted to anything is an addict. Now the question is how does one become an addict? Before you become an addict to anything, you have to go through a process. Nobody becomes addicted overnight. It is a gradual process which is true for both positive and negative addictions, but I will center on negative addictions. King Solomon reveals this process in Proverbs 1:10-14:

> *My son if sinners entice thee, consent thou not. If they say, Come with us, let us lay wait for blood, let us lurk privily to the innocent without cause. Let us swallow them up alive as the grave; and whole, as those that go down into the pit. We shall find all precious substance; we shall fill our houses with spoil. Cast in thy lot among us; let us all have one purse.*

Though the above passage gives us a vivid picture of peer pressure or gangs who engage in armed robbery, it reveals to us the process by which one can develop a destructive, addictive habit. There are four stages in this process.

1. Enticement to Experiment

An individual is completely innocent in relation to the addiction prior to becoming an addict. In order to become addicted to anything, one has to first have an experience with that thing. A drug addict becomes an addict because he first experienced it by innocently experimenting. The same is true with a person who experiments with sex and then becomes sexually promiscuous with many sexual partners. People experience or experiment things for the first time out of curiosity birthed from their own volition, but most of the time, they are enticed by someone else.

It can take just one person or a few friends to introduce a person into sin and place them on the journey to addiction. Satan, the tempter, uses people to tamper with the life of the innocent. Sinners love to sin and love to entice the innocent to sin with them.

To entice is to lure or seduce. It means "to lead away from accepted principles or proper conduct." It also means "to attract by arousing hope and desire."[4] In order to entice you, folks will advise you and devise strategies to get you to try their vices. God's advice however is this: *My son if sinners entice thee, consent thou not* (Proverbs 1:10).

---

4 Entice. 2013. In *TheFreeDictionary.com*. Retrieved July 1st, 2013, from www.thefreedictionary.com/entice

The one being enticed will say, "I have not done this before; I am afraid."

And the person doing the enticement will say something like, "There is always a first time, it will not hurt. It is pleasurable and fun. You will love it." He will use sweet words to promise pleasure and reward. Part of the enticement process is a promise of plunder or pleasure. However, the inevitable disastrous consequences are never mentioned.

> We shall find all precious substance, we shall fill our houses with spoil (Proverbs 1:13).

As I have pointed out, this passage refers to a gang or a group of armed robbers. As they outline their job description, you realize their activities are obviously dangerous, and one could easily lose his life by being a part of them. As you can see, the risk and perils are not disclosed. It's only the gains that are promised. That is what Satan does; he promises pleasure and gain and becomes silent on the wages of sin. One needs to stand firm. Choose well your company of friends.

Through the advertisement of their products firms and companies entice prospective customers. This explains why models, beautiful and half-naked women, are often used. In beer commercials on television, the bottle looks cool and refreshing, thus, enticing people to taste. But here is God's advice: *Look not thou upon the wine when it is red, when it giveth his colour in the cup, when it moveth itself aright* (Proverbs 23:31).

God says do not give in when you are being enticed. Do not yield to temptation. When you are not able to say no to temptation, and you experience or experiment for the first time, there is the probability it will evolve to a greater desire.

2. Experimentation Leads to Evolvement

The Bible describes the duration of the pleasures of sin as for a season in Hebrews 11:25: *Choosing rather to suffer affliction with the people of God, than to enjoy the **pleasures of sin for a season*** (emphasis mine).

Stolen waters are sweet and bread eaten in secret is pleasant (Proverbs 9:17).

Some sort of pleasure is derived in sinning, and that is one of the reasons some people are steeped or stuck in it. It will amaze you to know that even serial killers find some sort of pleasure in killing their victims. They are happy when their victims cry and beg them to spare their lives at gun point. Due to the pleasure gained in sin, a first-timer is tempted strongly to sin again and again.

By evolvement, I mean you desire more. Your first-time experience is an introduction that grows or evolves into a stronger desire. At this stage the excitement you gained from your first time triggers your appetite for more. You do not need anyone to pressure you anymore; the perceived pleasure you enjoyed the first time will put pressure on you to indulge in it again. At this point, no one violates your right by forcing you, but out of your own volition and will, you want to use it or do it again and again.

Sin may be pleasurable but do not forget that the pleasure is only for a season. It is temporal. That means it does not last so control your lust. As your experience evolves, you will get deeply involved.

3. Evolvement Leads to Involvement

Evolvement leads to involvement. At this stage, your desire grows. You get involved more and take an active part in a particular sin. You ask and look for more and become an abuser and habitual user. The number of times you indulge in that particular sin or evil activity increases. If it is fornication, you increase your tally of sexual partners. If it is smoking, the number of cigarette sticks or packs you smoke daily gradually rises. When you get actively involved, you are heading towards addiction.

4. Involvement Leads to Engrossment

Involvement leads to being engrossed and addicted to negative acts. Here, one becomes completely dependent on the thing he is addicted to. When you are engrossed, you give your time, money, energy, and attention to the thing you are addicted to.

> *Cast in thy lot among us; let us all have one purse* (Proverbs 1:14).

At the addiction stage, you become a partner or full member. Here you do things in common and have things in common. You are equally yoked together with your gang or group. At this stage, you also go around looking for disciples. That is to say, you entice other innocent souls to taste and start the journey on the road to addiction.

Common Addictions

Many lesser known negative addictions exist such as addiction to television, shopping, excessive spending, video games, food, and movies, but I have chosen to write about alcohol, drugs, pornography, and gambling because not only are they common, they are very, very destructive. Indulging in them can bring about serious and disastrous consequences that affect not only the addict but also the people who are connected with his life.

1. Alcohol Addiction

Alcohol has been a controversial issue in the Christian community. Some Christians argue there is nothing wrong with drinking alcohol as long as you do not get boozed. In his article titled "Alcohol and the Bible", James Boyd reiterated; "God's Word has been compared to a map showing us where the 'landmines' in life are." He then went ahead to point out that beverage alcohol is one of those landmines. If it is a landmine, then it has to be avoided at all cost before it causes havoc. In fact, total abstinence is the key and best policy.

When the Bible mentions wine, which in Hebrew is *yayin*, it refers to wine of every kind, fermented and unfermented. The term "strong drink," whose Hebrew word is *shekar*, is an intoxicating drink. Alcoholic wine and strong drink are, therefore, not good. Proverbs 23:29-35 backs this up:

> *Who hath woe? Who hath sorrow? Who hath contentions? Who hath babbling? Who hath wounds without cause? Who hath redness of eyes? They that tarry long at the wine; they that go to seek mixed wine. Look not thou upon the wine when it is red, when it giveth his colour in the cup, when it moveth itself aright. At the last it biteth like a serpent, and stingeth like an adder. Thine eyes shall behold strange women, and thine heart shall utter perverse things. Yea, thou shall be as he that lieth down in the midst of the sea, or as he that lieth upon the top of a mast. They have stricken me, shalt thou say, and I was not sick; they have beaten me; and I felt it not: when shall I awake? I will seek it yet again.*

The above passage is a vivid description of the life of a typical alcohol-addicted person. Why will alcohol intake result in sorrows (vv. 29-30), immorality (v. 33), insecurity (v. 34) insensitivity and insensibility (v. 35), and why was it even compared to a poisonous snake (v. 32). And yet, one will say I will seek it yet again? There is only one reason: addiction!

Whether you are an occasional drinker or an addicted drinker, the negative and awful things the Bible says about alcohol and its drinker should be enough to make you quit altogether. Putting the Bible and religion aside, the wreckage and havoc caused by it should be enough to help you make a wise decision.

Wine is a mocker, strong drink is raging: and whosoever is deceived thereby is not wise (Proverbs 20:1).

It is not for kings, O Lemuel, it is not for kings to drink wine nor for princes strong drink: lest they drink, and forget the law, and pervert the judgment of any of the afflicted (Proverbs 31:4-5).

> *Take it or leave it; anything you do secretly or hide to do for fear of what people will say is likely to be a sin against God.*

We are living epistles of Christ that all men read, therefore, we should be careful not to make them stumble. As a Christian, I do not want to be known as a drinker. Neither do I want to drink secretly. Take it or leave it; anything you do secretly or hide to do for fear of what people will say is likely to be a sin against God. Remember the Bible mentions secret sins.

2. Drug Addiction

Drug abuse or addiction is a big problem among both sexes of all ages. Drug addiction is a compelling urgency to acquire and use drugs. Drug abuse ultimately leads to drug addiction which ruins relationships, destroys health, and disrupts normal activities. We must say a big NO to drugs!

Let us refuse drugs the same way Jesus refused the wine mixed with bitter gall they offered Him while he hung on the cross in excruciating pain(Matthew 27:34). Some Bible commentators believe gall was a kind of drug.

3. Pornography Addiction

We are living in a world where temptation is everywhere, and apparently sexual temptation ranks on top. We are daily enticed by what we see on television, in the movies, on the internet, and on the streets. Men are more prone to this sin, as they are attracted by what they see.

Peter describes people who are addicted to lust or pornography in this way. *Having eyes full of adultery, and that cannot cease from sin* (2 Peter 2:14a). Their eyes just cannot cease from sin. They cannot stop visiting pornographic sites and are fond of watching X-rated movies. They cannot take their eyes and mind off an immodestly dressed woman.

It is a kind of addiction most people keep secret, and the tendency to hide it makes it more difficult to break the habit. For this reason it kills its victims slowly but surely.

It must be noted that pornography does not travel alone. It walks with other strong giants like fornication or illicit sex, sexual lust, and masturbation to mention a few. Why? Because you will definitely practice what you watch. It's unfortunate that pastors, men, women, young people, married couples, and singles are all trapped in pornography addiction and its accompanying addictions.

In the book *Every Young Man's Battle*, co-author Stephen Arterburn quoted Ed Cole as saying "Not only does pornography encourage its viewers to create an image in their minds. It also entices them to fantasize about it. Usually these fantasies involves an erotic act that can only be satisfied with someone else or by masturbation. Once an image develops in the mind, that picture creates a stronghold in the mind and becomes a trap."

The Bible is spot on about looking at the nakedness of somebody. Leviticus 20:17 tells us it is a wicked thing. It is also a shameful thing because nakedness in the Bible is associated with shame. However, between married couples, it is right and honorable. Married couples obviously are allowed to look at the nakedness of each other. However, they are not supposed to watch someone else's nakedness in a movie or video.

Watching pornographic pictures or movies is a sin! If looking on a well-dressed or half-naked woman to lust after her signifies committing adultery with her in your heart (Matthew 5:28), then pornography being a sin is unquestionable.

4. Gambling Addiction

And not many days after the younger son gathered all together, and took his journey into a far country, and there wasted his substance with riotous living (Luke 15:13).

Riotous living is very generic, and one of the things included in it is gambling. People gamble with the hope of getting rich overnight. God worked, and His will for man according to Genesis 3:17 is to work. The essence of work is not only the money we derive but also the help and enhancement it offers humanity or society. Gambling kills the discipline to work and the workers' discipline to save.

Let him that stole steal no more: but rather let him labour, working with his hands the thing which is good, that he may have to give to him that needeth (Ephesians 4:28).

If any would not work, neither should he eat (2 Thessalonians 3:10b).

5. Smoking Addiction

Countless number of people are addicted to smoking, be it tobacco, cigarettes, pipes, cigars or marijuana. The Bible is silent on smoking, but common sense and science prove that smoking can be dangerous to one's health. Tobacco smoking causes cancer and other heart related diseases.

On the cigarette pack, it is conspicuously written: "cigarette smoking can be harmful to your health" or "smoking can kill you." Smokers see this bold health warning, yet they cannot quit smoking. Why? They are addicted. Even medical doctors who know the health implications of smoking on their health do smoke.

> *Out of his mouth go burning lamps, and sparks of fire leap out. Out of his nostrils goeth smoke, as out of a seething pot or caldron* (Job 41:19-20).

The above Scripture is one of the descriptions of Satan as a dragon. The Bible tells us smoke comes out of his nostrils. We can therefore deduce that a smoker is little different from Satan. Your body is the temple of God in which the Holy Spirit dwells. Do not destroy your vital organs and your body as a whole by inhaling smoke.

How to be Set Free from Destructive Addictions

If you cannot heed the Spirit's plea to be holy, if you cannot flee from fornication, and if you still go on a drinking spree as a Christian, you are not truly free. You therefore need to be set free or come out of the bondage of addiction.

I must confess that addictive desires are so strong and intense that they cannot be overcome easily. Just as the addiction was not formed overnight, so it is not likely to go away overnight except by the power of the Holy Spirit. To be set free or delivered from addiction can be

SPIRITUAL VALUE SYSTEM

a herculean task for man but not for God. God specializes in setting the captives free. If the Son therefore shall set you free, you shall be free indeed. You may be an addict, but God's verdict is that every addiction can be evicted from your life for you to be totally free.

The principles below will go a long way to help you along the way.

- Be very honest and open to God about your situation.
- Confess that you cannot change yourself in any way and that you depend totally on Him to change you.
- While you make a concrete decision to leave your addictive lifestyle, cleave to the Lord Jesus Christ. Do not linger in your addiction anymore but cling onto Him. Change your friends and environment if necessary. By so doing, you avoid temptations. The best way to avoid temptation is to avoid temptation.

> *You may be an addict, but God's verdict is that every addiction can be evicted from your life for you to be totally free.*

- Replace negative addictions with positive or holy ones.
- Go through a process of counseling. Let someone who is spiritually strong and mature guide and mentor you.
- Find a trusted person you can be accountable to.
- Stick to the Word. Confess it all the time. You can confess the following Scriptures depending on your kind of addiction. I have purposed in my heart that I would not defile my body (Daniel 1:8); I have made a covenant with my eyes (Job 31:1); I will set no evil before my eyes (Psalm 101:3); I have purposed that my mouth shall not transgress (Psalm 17:3b); my body is the temple of God in which the Holy Spirit dwells (1 Corinthians 3:16).
- Go through deliverance. There are some kinds which cannot go except by fasting and prayers.

CHAPTER EIGHT

Becoming a God-Addict

We learned from the previous chapter that addiction is not always negative. As a matter of fact, people can be addicted in the positive sense. In the Scriptures, we read of a family with a very positive or if you like holy addiction.

> ...Ye know the house of Stephanas, that it is the first fruits of Achaia, and that they have addicted themselves to the ministry of the saints (1 Corinthians 16:15).

Other versions of the Bible translate *addicted* as "devoted." This family was devoted to or gave themselves habitually to serving the saints. They never missed an opportunity to do good to people. They were not forced to love, be hospitable, or be good to others. They did it wholeheartedly and deemed it a great privilege.

God wants us to be addicted to the things of God. In fact, any spiritual activities He commands us to do, He wants us to be addicted to them. He does not want us to be sporadic but rather consistent and addicted in the end. We are commanded in Scripture to pray, study the Bible, attend church, give, do good to people, and so on. When we are addicted to the above activities, then we can be called God-addicts.

Practicing the above Christian responsibilities may seem difficult and laborious, but when we become addicted through the help of the Holy Spirit, it will be more difficult for us not to do them than to do them.

I am going to show you certain Scriptures so you will realize that some words or phrases in them show that God wants us to be addicted to Him and to our Christian responsibilities.

Holy Habits

In 1996, the Coca Cola Company created an advertising slogan which goes: "Eat Football, Sleep Football, Drink Coca-Cola." This advertising campaign was tied in with the European 1996 Football Championships hosted by England. The fact is countless people are so addicted to the game of football or other sports that they literally eat it, drink it, sleep it and dream it. It is all they think and talk about.

God expects the believer to be addicted to spiritual and supernatural activities so they will literally eat, sleep, drink and dream them. The believer must form holy habits sustained and reinforced by the power of the Holy Ghost and the Word of God. You must be consistent, faithful, and resolute in obeying God in every area of life. This way you build up your resistance to change. Let us look at some of the specific things God wants us to be addicted to.

Addicted to The Word

The highlighted words and phrases (my emphasis) in the following Scriptures indicate that God wants us to be addicted to His Word.

> *These were more noble than those in Thessalonica, in that they received the word with all readiness of mind, and* **searched the scriptures daily,** *whether those things were so* (Acts 17:11).
>
> *This book of the law shall not* **depart** *out of thy mouth, but thou shall meditate therein* **day** *and* **night,** *that thou mayest observe to do according to all that is written therein: for*

then thou shalt make thy way prosperous and then thou shall have good success (Joshua 1:8).

Preach the Word; ***be instant in season, out of season;*** *reprove, rebuke, exhort with all longsuffering and doctrine* (2 Timothy 4:2).

For we will give ourselves ***continually*** *to prayer, and to the* ***ministry of the Word*** (Acts 6:4).

Searching the Word must be done daily; meditating upon the Word must be done day and night, and preaching the Word must be done in season and out of season or continually. The word that best describes our attitude to the activities mentioned above is addiction.

Now, the following Scripture sums up the attitude of any Word-addicted person. He prepares His heart to receive the Word (by hearing, reading, studying, eating, searching it), to do it (by obeying it), and teach it (propagating it via all mediums).

For Ezra had prepared his heart to seek the law of the LORD, and to do it, and to teach in Israel statutes and judgments (Ezra 7:10).

The first step towards Word addiction is eagerness and readiness to receive the Word through hearing, reading, studying and searching it. It's not enough to hear the Word taught or preached; you must open the Scriptures and search them for yourself. A church that practiced this discipline was the Berean church.

Luke commended the Bereans for their readiness to receive the Word and their discipline to search the Scriptures daily. These people were addicted to the Word of God which signifies daily addiction. Hearing the Word in the synagogue was not enough to quench their hunger for biblical truth, so they went the extra mile by searching the Word for themselves in their homes. God wants us to emulate them; thus, we prepare our hearts to receive the engrafted Word and search the Scriptures on a daily basis.

Many believers go to church to hear the Word, and when they get back home, they do not do any searching on what was taught and preached. Many do not even put down notes, and the few who write notes do not study their notes. Truly, saying that the Word of God has lost its relevance among believers is an understatement.

> *Truly, saying that the Word of God has lost its relevance among believers is an understatement.*

After receiving the Word, we are also expected to obey it daily through meditation, application, and living or doing it. Prosperity and good success comes from being addicted to the Word according to Joshua. After meditating and obeying what the Word instructs us, we are also supposed to preach and teach others. The Word-addicted person does not keep the Word to himself.

The preacher, as a herald of Christ, is supposed to be addicted to the Word by way of preaching it. Preacher, preach the Word in and out of season. If you want to witness miracles in your church or ministry, preach the Word. If you want to see breakthrough in your ministry, preach the Word. Never preach about yourself, your opinions, your theories, or what you think!

Lay members are also supposed to walk and talk the Word. When you are counseling or just talking to people, give them the Word. The Word is what people need, not your opinions. Be a Word addict.

The Bible says that all things were made by the Word, and there was nothing God made without the Word. In the same vein, any Word-addicted person does nothing without the Word. He advises and encourages people with the Word. He raises His family according to Scripture. He prays by quoting the Word. You will hear scriptural quotes in his everyday conversation. He makes wise choices by considering what the Word says. He simply eats the Word, thinks the Word, speaks the Word, and lives the Word.

Addicted To Prayer

> *We will give ourselves **continually** to **prayer** and to the ministry of the word* (Acts 6:4, emphasis mine).

> *Pray **without ceasing*** (2 Thessalonians 5:17, emphasis mine).

Apart from the Word, we need to be addicted to prayer. The word *continually* and the phrase "without ceasing" simply mean we are to be addicted to prayer. We should let prayer become our culture, our lifestyle, and part and parcel of us. The Bible is full of people who were prayer addicts: the apostles, Daniel, Elijah, Anna the prophetess, and Epaphras to mention but a few. Let's take a brief look at Daniel.

> *Now when Daniel knew that the writing was signed, he went into the house; and his windows being open in his chamber toward Jerusalem, he kneeled upon his knees **three times a day**, and prayed and gave thanks before his God **as he did aforetime*** (Daniel 6:10, emphasis mine).

When the people wanted to stop Daniel's praying, they made a royal statute and put into place a firm decree prohibiting prayer. The Bible says that Daniel defied the law and prayed three times a day to his God as he always did. Before the law, he prayed three times daily, and after the law, he did the same. Why? The answer is simple: he was simply addicted to prayer. It was his custom. Against his lifestyle of prayer, there was no law. Christians are prayerless today, because Satan has made a decree that they should not pray to their God.

The Psalmist David also developed a culture of prayer. Hear what he said in Psalm 55:17: *Evening and morning and at noon, will I pray, and cry aloud: and he shall hear my voice.*

This is addiction. All through the book of Psalms, we see David pray and talk often about prayer. In all situations, David loved to go to God in prayer – when he sinned, when he was afraid, when threatened by his enemies, when in need, when discouraged, and so on.

When God answers our prayers, people who are skeptical and critical about God and prayer call it a mere coincidence. But what we know is that when we stop praying, the so-called coincidence will also stop, and more accidents, incidents, and sicknesses will occur. We keep coming to God in prayer because He keeps hearing us.

O thou that heareth prayer, unto thee shall all flesh come (Psalm 65:2).

Addicted to Thanksgiving, Praising and Worshiping God

God requires these three things from us, and we are not to do them sporadically. They are to be done continuously and persistently. We thank Him for He is worthy; we praise Him for what He has done; and we worship Him for who He is. At what times? All the time!

In everything give thanks: *for this is the will of God in Christ Jesus concerning you* (1 Thessalonians 5:18, emphasis mine).

I will **bless the LORD at all times,** *His praise shall* **continually** *be in my mouth* (Psalm 34:1, emphasis mine).

By him therefore, let us offer the **sacrifice of praise to God continually,** *that is, the fruit of our lips giving thanks to his name* (Hebrews 13:15, emphasis mine).

It is easy to thank, worship, and praise God when everything seems to be going well in our lives. It seems a natural response. But can you offer what is due Him when things are not going well? I mean in difficult and tough times when the Devil seems to have a field day in your life. Can you do or offer a combination of these three things the Lord requires from you when going through a Job-like situation? Can you rejoice in the Lord when faced with a situation similar to that of Habakkuk?

> *Although the fig tree shall not blossom, neither shall fruit be in the vines; the labour of the olive shall fail, and the fields shall yield no meat; the flock shall be cut off from the fold, and there shall be no herd in the stalls: Yet I will rejoice in the Lord, I will joy in the God of my salvation* (Habakkuk 3:17-18).

It takes people who are addicted to giving thanks, praise and worship to rejoice in such awkward and hopeless situations. Folks who are not addicted to praise, allow sorrow to take the place of praise; those who are not addicted to giving thanks think of themselves and often complain; and those who are not addicted to worship worry in such situations. The reason why God says we should thank Him even in bad times is that He is able to work all things together for our good. He is able to turn the tables and prepare a table before us in the presence of our enemies when we thank, praise, and worship Him in difficult times.

Learn to praise God in the pit, prison, and valley.

Praise is a very powerful weapon for believers. When we praise God in difficult times, the enemy becomes confused and unable to sustain his attack on our lives. Learn to praise God in the pit, prison, and valley.

Addicted to Church Attendance

> *Not forsaking the assembling of ourselves together, as the manner of some is, but exhorting one another: and so much the more, as ye see the day approaching* (Hebrews 10:25, emphasis mine).

The writer of the book of Hebrews admonishes us not to absent ourselves from the gathering of the saints if we call ourselves Christians. He said while some are in the habit of being absent from the gathering of believers, we must form the habit of going to church. Attending church regularly makes you a church-addict.

Lots of Christians are fond of missing church, especially week-day, evening, prayer meetings and Bible studies. To such Christians, they think they do the church and God a great deal of favor by occasionally showing up in church on Sundays. They are of the view that the church needs them more than they need the church.

Today, it is amazing how some Christians allow little offences to stop them from going to church. Such Christians are not addicted to attending church, and they do not understand the benefits of going into the house of the Lord. The believer must be so addicted to church that he can say like David, *I was glad when they said unto me, Let us go into the house of the Lord* (Psalm 122:1), and *I will dwell in the house of the Lord forever* (Psalm 23:6b).

Some of the benefits of going into the house of the Lord are as follows.

- Fullness of joy and pleasure for evermore (Psalm 16:11)
- Edification

- Growing from strength to strength (Psalm 84:7)
- Obtain mercy and receive grace to help in time of need (Hebrew 4:16)
- Opportunity to serve and exercise your spiritual gifts

Addicted to Giving

Giving is another Christian responsibility we are required to be addicted to. We should be consistent in giving tithes, offerings, alms to the needy, and in all kinds of giving. The Philippian church is an example of a church addicted to giving.

> *Now ye Philippians know also, that in the beginning of the gospel, when I departed from Macedonia, no church communicated with me as concerning **giving and receiving, but ye only.** For even in Thessalonica ye sent **once and again unto my necessity*** (Philippians 4:15-16, emphasis mine).

How do we know that this church was addicted to giving? The answer is clear in the verses above. The fact that they alone communicated to Paul about giving and receiving shows they were interested in the matter. And we know they were addicted to giving because they gave again and again.

All the other churches probably talked to Paul only on one side of the coin. They gave, but the church in question was eager to understand both sides of the coin so they asked questions to that effect. They wanted to know the best way to give in order to receive, so that giving and receiving could be a continuous cycle. If you only give without receiving, you will either be discouraged to continue giving or become replete of resources to give again. In that case, you will not be an addicted giver!

Paul likened the giving of the church to sweet-smelling perfume, acceptable and well-pleasing unto God and went ahead to say a very powerful prayer from his heart for them. We are always quick to quote, confess, and pray the prayer Paul prayed for the Philippians without emulating their exceptional example and attitude towards giving.

> *But my God shall supply all your need according to his riches in glory by Christ Jesus* (Philippians 4:19).

Concerning money and giving, attitude is very important. We must not have wrong attitudes like the rich young ruler who loved his money more than he loved the Lord. We must not emulate Judas Iscariot who, because he was fond of money, became a thief and condemned giving bountifully to the Lord as a waste. The attitude of Ananias and Sapphira who lied about their giving must be shunned.

Rather, we should strive to imitate the attitude of somebody like Barnabas who gave generously, liberally, and free-heartedly. The attitude of the poor widow towards giving is worth emulating as she gave sacrificially and truly gave according to how God had prospered her. Finally, the attitude of David towards giving was very challenging as he said in 2 Samuel 24:24 that he would not give unto the Lord his God anything that cost him nothing.

Do not just be a cheerful giver, be an addicted giver!

Addicted to Doing Good

As Christians, though we have not been called due to our good works, we are called for good works. The covenant promise is that we shall be blessed to be a blessing unto others. And as God is committed to blessing us, we must be addicted to being a blessing unto others.

> *And let us **not be weary in well doing**: for in due season we shall reap, **if we faint not*** (Galatians 6:9, emphasis mine).

Not be weary in well doing and to *faint not,* suggest persistence which causes addiction. Now, two main factors can discourage a Christian from continuing to do good to people. One is ungratefulness on the part of people we have helped in the past, and the other is not reaping the blessings in giving.

Even God expects to hear "thank you Lord" otherwise Jesus would not have questioned and queried the whereabouts of the other nine, ungrateful, healed lepers. That tells you that an expression of appreciation can boost one's morale to continue with a good gesture. Having said that, in our world today, if you do good to anybody, do not expect to be thanked; otherwise you may have the shock of your life. Though an attitude of gratitude is good, it should not be that which fuels you to do more for people in these end times. You want to know why? Paul mentioned ungratefulness as one of the end-time apostate behaviors of man in the book of Timothy. Men will be ungrateful to God and fellow men.

If ungratefulness on the part of someone discourages you from helping anybody again, the risk is that an angel may sooner or later knock at your door, and you will fail to offer any assistance within your means. Never put all men into one bracket because of bad experiences you had with one or a few people. Never say never!

> *Be not forgetful to entertain strangers: for thereby some have entertained angels unawares (Hebrews 13:2).*

You have no excuse. Paul's admonition is that as long as we have the opportunity to do good to people we should endeavor to seize it.

> *As we have therefore opportunity, let us do good unto all men, especially unto them who are of the household of faith (Galatians 6:10).*

As we have the opportunity, the possibility, the means, the resources, the strength, the ability, we should go ahead and bless people without taking into account the ingratitude of people in the past. Besides that, when we do not realize the blessings in giving, we should not let that hinder us from giving more to more. Look, there is a Scriptural promise:

> *Cast not away therefore your confidence, which hath great recompense of reward. For ye have need of patience, that, after ye have done the will of God, ye might receive the promise* (Hebrews 10:35-36).

After you have done the will of God by helping people, you need to exercise a great deal of patience. Your reward will be a done deal. Be addicted to doing good no matter what!

It has been said that the best way to overcome negative addictions is to replace them with good ones. I pray you replace your worldliness with the Word, talking to men and gossiping with addiction to prayer and intercession, worry and anxiety with thanksgiving, praises and worship, dwelling in the tents of wickedness with dwelling in the house of God forever, and being at the receiving end with being at the giving end.

May the popular saying "once an addict, always an addict" hold true in your life in a positive sense. Be loosed from any bad addiction and become a God-addict for good!

CHAPTER NINE

Hungry and Thirsty for God

There is a strong correlation between what you are hungry for and what you are addicted to. Whatever you are addicted to, you are always hungry or thirsty for. There can be no addiction without hunger or thirst. To be thirsty, hungry, desirous, or long and yearn for someone or something are all strong and forceful tugs on our psyches. They are not like wishing for something; wishing is weak and passive.

> *Desire drives us, hunger causes us to hurry, but just wishing makes us sit and tarry.*

Desire drives us, hunger causes us to hurry, but just wishing makes us sit and tarry.

Biblically speaking, hunger, thirst, and longing are mostly used for God, while desire is used for things, be it the things of God, the things of the flesh, or the world.

> *Therefore, I say unto you, what things soever ye desire, when ye pray, believe that ye receive them and ye shall have them* (Mark 11:24).

Whenever a desire or hunger is present, actions like prayer, fasting, seeking, and knocking certainly follow. In the natural, unless one is hungry and thirsty, one will not look for food and water. Until one has a desire, one will not aspire.

Similarly, we will not pursue God and the things of God if we are not hungry and thirsty for them. In many places in the Bible, you come across the words *hunger, thirst,* or *desire*. You will also in the same context see the word *come* which is an invitation or a decision to pursue, implying we cannot seek or come to God without first being hungry or thirsty for Him. Simply put, hunger and thirst draws us toward God.

For instance, *If any man thirst, let him come unto me* (John 7:37). *Ho everyone that thirsteth, come* (Isaiah 55:1) *and the spirit and the bride say, Come . . . And let him that is athirst come* (Rev 22:17).

The Tree, Wilderness, Desolate and Waste Grounds Have Hope

God has made promises to pour rain on a tree that has been cut down, the wilderness, the desolate ground and the waste ground. This offers hope in spite of their situation.

> *For there is hope of a tree, if it be cut down, that it will sprout again, and that the tender branch thereof will not cease. Though the root thereof wax old in the earth and the stock thereof die in the ground. Yet through the scent of water it will bud, and bring forth boughs like a plant* (Job 14:7-9).

God has also promised *to cause it to rain on the earth, where no man is; on the **wilderness**, wherein there is no man; to satisfy the **desolate** and **waste ground**; and to cause the bud of the tender herb to spring forth* (Job 38:26, 27, emphasis mine).

If these have hope, you can rest assured there is hope for you, too; regardless of how dry and desolate you may be spiritually. For your information, you are far better than a tree, the wilderness and a dry ground. Your body is the temple of God. You were created in the image of God. You are a child of God.

It is the serious intention of God to fill us with Himself. That makes God our hope, and we the people of hope through Jesus. Christ in you, the hope of glory. The prerequisite to have this experience is to desire, hunger, and thirst for God. God has an obligation Himself to satisfy the incessant and insistent hunger and thirst of people who come to Him.

> *Blessed are they which do hunger and thirst after righteousness: for they shall be filled* (Matthew 5:6).

Evidences of a Hungry and Thirsty Life

In the book of Psalms, we see how thirsty and hungry the Psalmist David and others were for God. They were not hungry and thirsty for physical things that satisfy temporarily but for God and spiritual things. They beautifully expressed and penned it. The following Psalms are a few examples.

> *As the hart panteth after the water brooks, so panteth my soul after thee, O God. My soul thirsteth for God, for the living God: when shall I come and appear before God? My tears have been my meat day and night, while they continually say unto me* **Where is thy God?** (Psalm 42:1-3, emphasis mine).

> *O God, thou art my God;* **early will I seek thee**, *my soul thirsteth for thee, my flesh longeth for thee in a dry and thirsty land, where no water is; to see thy power and thy glory, so as I have seen thee in the sanctuary* (Psalm 63:1-2, emphasis mine).

One thing have I desired of the Lord, that will I seek after; **that I may dwell in the house of the Lord all the days of my life,** *to behold the beauty of the Lord and to enquire in his temple* (Psalm 27:4, emphasis mine).

These three different Psalms show us four things evident in a life longing for God. If these four elements are absent, it means we are not hungry for more of God. Anyone who is hungry for God has a **quest;** that is, he searches or pursues God until he finds Him. He also has **questions;** he asks questions as to when and where he can find God and how he can know God better. He is **quick;** he does not delay in seeking and obeying God. Finally, he receives **queries** from enemies and skeptics in their attempt to mock and scorn him. I pray that as you read this book, an intense spiritual hunger will be created within your soul and spirit for you to seek God like never before. May you thirst for His Spirit, presence, power, and holiness.

QUEST: Desire to Dwell in the House of the Lord Always

David, the man after God's own heart, points out that he desires one thing: to dwell in the house of the Lord forever. He continues to say that the reason he wants to dwell in the house of the Lord is to behold the beauty of the Lord and to enquire in His temple. In other words, he wants to have the benefits of abiding in the house of the Lord.

It's important to note that David narrowed his desires to just one thing. Until we narrow our desires to one thing and single it out, we are not truly thirsty or hungry. If our choices and focuses are many, we do not truly have a desire.

Like David, we must have a strong desire to dwell in the house of the Lord all the days of our lives. Going to church goes a long way to help a Christian mature. You are not in Christ because you are in church, but if you are truly in Christ, you will be in church. How often you go to church depends on your hunger and thirst for God. As you linger in His presence all the time, you will never lack His presence at any time. If you are thirsty for God, you will make His house your second home, and He will make your heart His home.

> *My soul longeth, yea even fainteth for the courts of the LORD, my heart and my flesh crieth out for the living God. Yea the sparrow hath found an house, and the swallow a nest for herself, where she may lay her young, even thine altars, O LORD of hosts, my King and my God. Blessed are they that dwell in thy house: they will be still praising thee. Selah* (Psalm 84:2-4).

Anyone who is hungry for God is eager to be in the presence of the Lord or dwell in the house of the Lord. Such a person is glad when he is told "let us go into the house of the Lord." If a Christian starts neglecting going to church, it is a sign they have lost their appetite for God and the things of God.

QUESTION: When Shall I Come and Appear Before God?

"When shall I come and appear before God?" is the question of one who is hungry and thirsty for God. That is to say, even while a God-thirsty person is still in the presence of God, he is thinking of having yet another encounter with Him. Such a person can never come to the place where he is so satisfied with His presence that he would not need another experience. He is simply addicted to church or God's presence. He loves to be in His presence, either alone in his closet or in the gathering of the saints, worshiping God in the beauty of His holiness. He loves to praise, worship, and commune with his Maker.

Nowadays because of coldness of heart, a lukewarmness, and lack of hunger in the heart of many Christians, they expect the pastor or the church to ask them when they will come to church. If you do not actively seek to know when there will be church, but expect to be asked when you will come to church, it is a sign that you are lukewarm. If you do not join fellow believers in fellowship, but expect them to follow up on you, you are not hungry for God. If you do not enquire, but require the church to query why you have stopped coming to church, you lack desire at best, and you are a backslider at worst.

> *If you do not enquire, but require the church to query why you have stopped coming to church, you lack desire at best, and you are a backslider at worst.*

> *Not forsaking the assembling of ourselves together, as the manner of some is; but exhorting one another and so much the more, as ye see the day approaching* (Hebrews 10:25).

Many a time, when you attempt to evangelize someone or invite the person to church, they are very quick to say "I am already a Christian and to me, going to church is not that important." The Scripture the Devil gives them to defend or support their stance is that God looks at the heart. Christianity is a matter of the heart, they allege. Those folks are either backslidden, religious, or simply lack the desire to draw near to God. Going to church does not make you a Christian, but the truth is, if you are a Christian, you will go to church.

Right from the first day after I was born again (which happened to be a Sunday), I attended two services continuously for three years, before I left my home country and changed churches. I walked a long distance to and from church, as money for transportation sometimes was a problem. I was in every weekday, evening meeting and sometimes remained after service in order to pray all night alone or with friends. Saturday was the only day I was not in church because there was no meeting. I was supposed to attend a new convert class for six months, but I repeated the class for more than a year and became a teaching assistant.

I could not wait to attend the next service even while I was in one. My first love was intact, and my hunger for God incessant. I thank God that I am still hungry to know Him more and more.

Apart from the fact that I was thirsty for God, I also knew I needed the church more than the church needed me, because the Devil who was after my life was so real. When I became born again, I did not need someone to follow-up on me. I knew I needed to take up my cross and follow Christ. Some believers erroneously believe that the church needs them more than they need the church. They want to be begged before they step foot in the house of God. To them, attending a church service is tantamount to doing the church a great service. Little do they realize that missing a church service is actually a disservice to themselves. Now, let me ask, between the worshipper and the One worthy of worship, who loses or benefits? If you fail to approach God, He will raise up stones to do what you were supposed to do, and the benefit you could have enjoyed is lost.

I pray that you will be so hungry for God that anytime you are in His presence, either privately or in a church setting, you will be asking, "When shall I come and appear before my God again!" It means when you are in church on a Sunday morning, you are eager to find out when the next meeting is scheduled. You will ask and enquire gladly, "Will there be a midweek service, prayer meeting, or Bible studies?" It shows your readiness to come into His presence to worship, learn, and receive more of Him and from Him. Do not be a Sunday-only or an occasional church-goer.

QUICKNESS: Early Will I Seek Thee

Anyone hungry for God seeks God early. First of all, he remembers his Creator and repents in the days of his youth. He does not postpone his decision to give his life to Christ (Ecclesiastes 12:1). Secondly, he seeks God in the Word and prayer early in the morning. That means he is serious with his quiet time or morning devotion. Thirdly, he seeks to do the will of God early because he knows he must do the will of God while it is day, for the night comes when no man can work. Such a person knows that delayed obedience is equal to disobedience (Psalm 119:60). Finally, he is never late for church and that's the point I am going to elaborate on.

> *I love them that love me; and those that seek me early shall find me* (Proverbs 8:17).

> *And ye shall seek me, and find me, when ye shall search for me with all your heart* (Jeremiah 29:13).

In order for our quest to find God to be more than a mirage, the Bible gives us two conditions: (1) seeking Him with all our **heart,** and (2) seeking him **early.** We have no argument with how important our heart is in our relationship with God. What we do not pay attention to is the right timing with which we are to seek Him and do His will.

A Christian who is hungry for God is not the one who is always in church, but the one who is always in church early. He is the one who is never late, not just the one who is present on every date. He is the one who is punctual, not merely the one whose attendance is continual. He is the one who is always on time, not just the one who goes to church every time.

To avoid lateness, you need to prepare your attire on Saturday evening. If you iron your clothes on Sunday mornings, you are likely to be late, and it's not a good sign of someone who is hungry for God and desires to seek Him early.

> *My soul waiteth for the Lord more than they that watch for the morning: I say more than they that watch for the morning* (Psalm 130:6).

If you are looking forward to going to an important place, hearing good news, or meeting an important person the next morning, you can hardly wait. In the evening, or night, you prepare mentally, emotionally, and physically and eagerly await the next morning with expectation. Our preparation to go to an important place like the church, to hear the good news of the Word, and to meet a very important person like God Himself must be done in the same manner. The Bible tells us that when we come to mount Zion, which is symbolic of the church, God the Judge of all, Jesus the Mediator of the new covenant, innumerable company of angels, and the like are present (Hebrews 12:22-24).

Lateness is a big problem for most churches, especially among African churches, whether in Africa or abroad. Being a proud African myself, I must admit we are notorious for a lack of respect for time. I once heard my mentor, Rev. Eastwood Anaba, tell a story about when he was a guest speaker for a revival meeting in an African-dominated church in Germany. When his host was giving the announcement at the close of the first night, he said, "Tomorrow the meeting starts 4:00 p.m. for Africans and 6:00 p.m. for Europeans. My mentor became confused a bit and later asked his friend if there would be two services. His host explained. "If I mention 6:00 p.m., our people will come at 8:00 p.m. So 4:00 p.m. is 6:00 p.m. for them. It is ridiculous but serious!

We are rarely late for work, but when it comes to church, we are often really late. Whatever we agree on earth is agreed in heaven so when a meeting is scheduled at a particular time, heaven approves it and therefore dispatches angels to count and write names or keep records of those who arrive on time.

> *The LORD shall count when he writeth up the people, that this man was born there. Selah. As well the singers as the players on instruments shall be there: all my springs are in thee* (Psalm 87:6, 7).

When you listen to testimonies of people whom God gave the privilege to see heaven and return, you realize almost all of them mentioned that angels are present at church services to take record of those who are on time. The above Scripture gives us a revelation that God writes and counts and urges singers and players to be there on time. What about the congregation and the ministers? See this.

> *Bless ye the LORD, all ye his hosts; ye ministers of his, that do his pleasure* (Psalm 103:21).

The hosts refer to the congregation, and the ministers obviously are pastors, preachers, and others in service to the Lord. This psalm is telling us that ministers ought to join the congregation to participate in praises and worship. As much as members come to church late, I have a big problem with ministers of the gospel, especially guest speakers, turning up late.

It is a common practice for ministers and guest preachers to come to meetings or church late. They are on time in respect to the time allotted them to minister, but many do not respect the time the service starts. By the time they enter the hall amidst body guards, opening prayer, praises, and worship are over. It looks like they are so anointed that they are above bowing down to the Lord God almighty in worship. If our boss, the Holy Spirit, is present from the beginning of the service, who are we to be late intentionally? Whenever I am invited to minister, I always insist that my host makes sure I am brought early to the church. If God stooped and bowed down as it were to man during the creation of man, nothing stops any man from bowing down to God in worship.

QUERY: Where Is Thy God?

When crying, weeping, mourning and groaning become a pattern in your life, it means you are far from experiencing the fullness of joy. And when your enemies and those skeptical about God see this, they will ask, "Where is thy God?" They are not asking for you to show them the way to your God, rather they point to the fact that by your example your God does not exist. They are not asking because they want to follow your God. Instead they want to mock you and your God. When miracles are not seen in your life, ridicule from your enemies is inevitable.

They ask this question to mock you, because in their view your experiences do not line up with your profession of the greatness of your God and what He is capable of doing. Friend, the fact is if your prayers go unanswered, your life and situation seem to remain the same to those around you. To them it appears you are not making headway in life. Your enemies will make fun of you and your God whom they do not believe in. Such a question and mockery from skeptics and enemies should arouse a person's hunger for God, and the determination to believe God for a change.

For all the days of my appointed time, will I wait till my change comes (Job 14:14).

Your enemies are mocking you, but have the patience. Wait until your change comes. Continue to trust in God and wait on Him. Do not be envious of the prosperity of the wicked and don't follow their evil ways. Live in the fear of the Lord all the time. In God's time, your change will come. God is preparing a table before you in the presence of your enemies. Those who thought you were a reproach will soon approach you, and you will extend grace to those who thought you were a disgrace.

The palmist said they continually ask where is thy God? I pray your enemies will never stop asking you that question. While all along they ask in order to mock you, eventually they will ask because they want you to show them, so they, can also follow Him. When this happens your enemies will ask you "what must we do?" and your response will be "repent!" At that time your enemies forsake their wicked ways and follow your God. May God bless you in such a way that your life will be an attraction to them. Receive beauty for ashes and a spirit of heaviness for the spirit of praise in Jesus name.

CHAPTER TEN

Tips on How to Have a Spiritual Value System

Through the previous nine chapters, I have sought to explain what it means to place premium on spiritual things rather than natural things. In this final chapter, I want to briefly share with you some nuggets on how you can develop a spiritual value system.

Be Spiritually Minded. Do not be carnally minded.

> *For to be carnally minded is death; but to be spiritually minded is life and peace. Because the carnal mind is enmity against God: for it is not subject to the law of God, neither indeed can be. So then they are in the flesh cannot please God* (Romans 8:6-8).

Let the Presence of God be Your Focus. Place a premium on it, not as a pretense but the real thing. Seek His presence to create a difference in your life. When you always abide in His presence in prayer, worship, the Word, and living a holy life, you will be a carrier of His presence. Moses asked for it and had it. You also ought to ask for it.

> *And he said unto him, if thy presence go not with me, carry us not up hence. For wherein shall it be known here that I and thy people have found grace in thy sight? Is it not in that thou goest with us? So shall we be separated, I and thy people from all the people that are upon the face of the earth* (Exodus 33:15-16).

Exercise Yourself Spiritually. Spiritual exercise has far greater value than physical exercise. The benefits of exercising physically are many; you get in shape, have a healthier body, probably live longer, look more attractive, develop more stamina, feel better about yourself, and are able to relate to others with more confidence.

To exercise physically is good, but it's far better to be concerned with spiritual exercise. The profit derived from bodily exercise is little compared with spiritual exercise. Spiritual exercise profits much. It has promise in this life and transcends to eternity. Much time, however, must be devoted to spiritual exercise and less time to physical exercise. If the reverse or opposite becomes the case, you will be physically strong but spiritually weak. The Devil is not afraid of someone who has spent time building up his muscles to become a giant physically but is spiritually a dwarf.

> *But refuse profane and old wives' fables and exercise thyself rather unto godliness. For bodily exercise profiteth a little: but godliness is profitable unto all things, having promise of the life that now is, and that which is to come* (1 Timothy 4:7-8).

Store Treasures in Heaven, Not on Earth.

> *Lay not up for yourselves treasures upon the earth, where moth and rust doth corrupt, and where thieves break through and steal. But lay up for yourselves treasures in heaven, where neither moth nor rust doth corrupt, and where thieves do not break through nor steal* (Matthew 6:19-20).

Jesus was admonishing His disciples in the above Scripture to not lay up treasures upon the earth. By this, He meant they should not grab material things on earth without using them to win souls into the kingdom. The purpose of all kingdom prosperity is to build the kingdom of God.

> *Cry yet, saying, Thus saith the Lord of hosts; My cities through prosperity shall yet be spread abroad; and the LORD shall yet comfort Zion, and shall yet choose Jerusalem* (Zechariah 1:17).

We must not forget the reason for which God blesses us; it is to invest in His kingdom and the apex of all kingdom investment is to ensure souls are won. If we store all our wealth in banks or consume it on our lusts, we lay up treasures on the earth. The safety of treasures stored up in heaven is guaranteed but those on earth are not. They are at the mercy of moth, rust, thieves, fire outbreak, recession, and natural disasters. Thieves and rust refer to satanic forces that devour earthly prosperity.

Let Bearing the Fruits of the Spirit be Your Priority Over Exercising the Gifts of the Spirit. You cannot have gifts without first having fruits. It is out of our fruits that we can have gifts to give away to bless others. The Holy Spirit is deposited in the believer as a seed, and He first and foremost bears fruits so we can have gifts to bless others. To this end, do not desire the gifts more than the fruits. Do not pray for the gifts at the expense of the fruits. The gifts can take you to places, but it's the fruits that give you stability in the faith and life in general. The gifts cannot take you to heaven. The gifts are about your charisma but the fruits are about your character.

> *The gifts can take you to places, but it's the fruits that give you stability in the faith and life in general.*

SPIRITUAL VALUE SYSTEM

> *But the fruit of the Spirit is love, joy, peace, longsuffering, gentleness, goodness, faith. Meekness, temperance: against such there is no law* (Galatians 5:22-23).

Give Your Tithe or Set it Aside First Before Making Your Tight Financial Budget. People whose value system is spiritual, like Abraham and Jacob, are diligent tithe-givers. Right from creation, God has tried to keep man away from greediness as is evident in the instruction that man could eat fruit from all the trees in the Garden but not from the Tree of the Knowledge of Good and Evil. Furthermore, man was instructed to use six days to work and set one day apart to serve and worship God. In the same vein, He requires us to give Him only ten percent of our income and enjoy the rest.

Today, there is so much hardship that families and individuals are unable to make ends meet. Before then, the strategy for managing personal finances could be called "operation live within your means," but now, it ought to be called "live below your means." As you try to live below your means, your financial budget will be very tight. Failure to tithe will make your tight finances tighter. Aside from giving your tithe, show compassion by giving alms and help to the poor and needy, good offerings to the Lord, and so on. Leave nothing undone.

> *Bring ye all the tithes into the storehouse, that there may be meat in mine house, and prove me now herewith, saith the Lord of hosts, if I will not open you the windows of heaven, and pour you out a blessing that there shall not be room enough to receive it* (Malachi 3:10).

> *...these ought ye to have done, and not to leave the other undone* (Matthew 23:23c).

Consider God's Business (the Kingdom Business) More Important Than Your Own Business. Deem the harvest field more important than your backyard garden. The Bible points out that everyone seeks his own and not that which is Christ's. Do not neglect kingdom business in order to go about your own business. Do not consider saving money more important than saving souls. Sow into souls. Go for souls. In spite of your occupation, winning souls must be your preoccupation. It is part of the work of God that Jesus talked about in John 9:4: *I must work the works of him that sent me while it is day: the night cometh when no man can work.*

Seek to Please God Alone and Not Man. As a matter of fact, you cannot even please men. So never try. Let all attempts to please people cease. When you say or do things to please someone, he may later tell you it should have been another way. In your attempt to please people, they will often be dissatisfied in the end.

When John the Baptist came neither eating nor drinking, the people said he had a devil. One would have thought the people would be happy and pleased with Jesus since He came to do the opposite of what John did. Ironically, they were not pleased with Him either and rather called Him names.

"What do I do then?" you may ask. Do what is right and live on the strength of your convictions. Do not be bothered by public and popular opinion. Do what pleases God. Do His will without apology to anyone.

> *That ye might walk worthy of the Lord unto all pleasing, being fruitful in every good work and increasing in the knowledge of God* (Colossians 1:10).

> *But as we were allowed of God to be put in trust with the gospel, even so we speak; not as pleasing men, but God, which trieth our hearts* (1 Thessalonians 2:4).

Obey God and Not Man. Let it be your single aim to obey God alone in every area of your life, not man. Respect men and honor them but do not obey them by going contrary to God's Word. Every now and then, man and situations will demand you live and act contrary to the Word of God, but always remember to let your yes be yes and your no be no. May you receive the boldness of the apostles when you are torn between obeying God or men!

> *But Peter and John answered and said unto them, Whether it be right in the sight of God to hearken unto you more than unto God, judge ye* (Acts 4:19).

Be a Lover of God More than a Lover of Pleasure. Love the Lord your God with all your heart, with all your soul, and with all your mind. Love godly pleasure rather than the pleasures of sin. Love the Creator more than His creation.

> *...lovers of pleasures more than lovers of God* (2 Timothy 3:4b).

Set Your Affections on Things Above

After the resurrection of Christ, He ascended to sit on the right hand of God. From the spiritual point of view, the believer is seated with Christ and must therefore live his or her life from that view point. The believer must set his affections on things above and seek them.

> *In the same way, a heavenly perspective shows us earthly things are insignificant.*

When you are in a plane, the higher it goes, the smaller and more insignificant things we value on earth appear. In fact, big things we toil for like houses, buildings, and cars look like toys. In the same way, a heavenly perspective shows us earthly things are insignificant.

If ye then be risen with Christ, seek those things which are above, where Christ sitteth on the right hand of God. Set your affection on things above, not on things on the earth (Colossians 3:1- 2).

Set Your Priorities Right. Put God and the things of God first in your life.

Seek ye first the kingdom of God, and his righteousness, and all these things shall be added unto you (Matthew 6:33).

Walk by Faith not By Sight. Do not let your life be influenced and controlled by the things you see, situations, and circumstances. Walk by faith. Be moved by the Word of God only.

For we walk by faith, not by sight (2 Corinthians 5:7).

Love Not the World, Neither the Things that Are in the World. John, the apostle of love, mentions two kinds of love and compares and contrasts them: the love of the world and the love for God. If a person is in a love web with the world, the love for God automatically goes to its lowest ebb. The opposite is also true.

Love not the world, neither the things that are in the world, if any man love the world, the love of the father is not in him (1 John 2:15).

You may ask, what in the world does the word *world* mean? World is mentioned several times in the Bible and has four distinct meanings. The first meaning is derived from the Greek word *cosmos* which refers to the physical earth. This is what Luke was talking about in Acts 17:24 when he wrote *God that made the world and all things therein*. Jesus was referring to everywhere on the globe when He said *Go ye into all the world* (Mark 16:15).

The second meaning refers to the inhabitants of the earth or the human race as in John 3:16: *For God so loved the world.*

Thirdly, the Bible uses the word *world* for those people who are alienated from God and are against the course of Christ. Unbelievers, non-Christians, or children of the Devil are also known as the world. In John 15:18, when Jesus said *if the world hate you,* He was pointing to them. The last meaning of the word *world* is the world system and that is what John, in our text, warns us not to love.

Have spiritual value system!

About The Book

We are to prioritize spiritual things since they are more beneficial and important than physical or earthly things. Unfortunately, the opposite is often the case in our lives since the latter are visible and more appealing to our senses. The purpose of this book is to arouse your appetite for spiritual things. It will teach you to stop chasing things of the earth and seek first the kingdom of God and His righteousness. It will change you from being natural, carnal, or religious to become spiritual and supernatural through the power of God's Word. You will be changed from being earthly minded to become heavenly or spiritually minded. In short, this book will help revive you to become the spiritual giant you ought to be.

Just as various systems function in the body to give us life, a *Spiritual Value System* will also make you spiritually alive.

This is a must-read for the believer and the unbeliever alike. Unbelievers will see the need to be born again. The backslider will return to the place of grace one more time, and the believer will move on to a new spiritual dimension in their walk with the Lord.

If you are ready to stop being halfhearted and lackadaisical in your attitude towards the things of God, ready to pursue God with great inner tenacity, physical purity, moral integrity, and spiritual intensity, *Spiritual Value System* is for you. Read *Spiritual Value System* and you will develop a spiritual value system!

About The Author

Julius Owusu is the founder and president of *Crying Voice International* (CVI), an evangelistic and revival itinerary ministry with a mission to set people free and set them ablaze for Christ. He is an author, song writer, conference speaker, and forthright preacher of the Word with signs and wonders following. The temperature of his message runs hot – very hot!

Having been trained in marketing, Julius realized his life-long mission is not to promote corruptible goods and services but rather to preach the incorruptible Word of God and promote the kingdom of God. He is passionate about his calling and faithful to the One who has called him.

He is the vice president of the Inter-denominational Youth for Change, an organization which seeks to empower young people in Italy and beyond.

Julius is married to Princess and blessed with a pair of cuties, Julian and Lois. They live in Modena, Italy and attend the Pilgrim Christian Church, where he serves in leadership.

To book or invite Revivalist Julius to speak in your church or conference, please write to us: *cryingvoiceint@gmail.com* or call: +39 3890132734 or +39 0594821667 (Italy) or +47 46392174 (Norway)

Contact us on Facebook: facebook.com/julius.owusu

Follow our blog: juliusowusu.blogspot.com

Notes

Notes

Notes

Notes

Notes

Notes

Notes

Notes

Notes

Notes

Notes

Notes

Notes